TENNIS AS A WISDOM PRACTICE

A Story About The Quest for Mastery

CARL FRANKEL

MANGO GARDEN

"Youth, large, lusty

loving, youth full of

grace, force, fascination,

Do you know that old Age

may come after you with

equal grace, force,

fascination?"

Leaves of Grass,
Walt Whitman (1819-1892)

©2022 Carl Frankel / Mango Garden Press

Cover and Interior Design: Erin Papa/The Turning Mill

ISBN: 9798437709672

Mango Garden Press

For more information:
PracticeofTennis.com

To Donna —

Thank you for your friendship —
and may all of your guests be
successful!

Carl

Acknowledgements

Thanks to the following friends old and new, with a preemptive apology to those I've not mentioned through a failure of memory …

Family and close friends: Susan and Woody Hunter, Eric Booth, Rob Lederer, Mitchell Ditkoff, Hud Talbott, Dan Getman, Deb Bansemer, Michael Carrigan, more.

My local tennis gang: Bill, Evan, Gary, Gustavo, Jake, James, Joe, Karen, Marco, Mark, Matt, TN, Tate, Tom, the three Riches, Wyatt, and others too many to mention.

Tennis pals who don't quite fit anywhere else: Bob Bernstein, Henry Kennedy, Doug Grunther, Ravi Ramaswami, Mitch Adler.

My new friends from SuperSeniorVille: Bob Angel, Joe Bouquin, Gary Chafetz, Lloyd Clareman, Bruce Crumley, George Deptula, Allen Geraci, Steve Gottlieb, Michael Harvey, Marshall Hubsher, Tom Jaklitsch, Gary Jenkins, Francis Kreysa, Jay Lubker, Vishnu Maharaj, Mark Morales, Jim Nelson, Ed Paige, Sonny Perkins, Denny Posteraro, Alec Roberts, Phil Roholt, Henry Steinglass, John Tashiro, Tommy Walker, Joe Touzin, Jon Wilson. And, I'm sure, more.

(To those on the above list who beat me:

Thanks for nuthin', buster.)

The great tennis players who have inspired me over the years: The mustachioed John Newcombe, the slender Ken Rosewall, the saintly Arthur Ashe, the sprightly Evonne Goolagong, our Lord God Roger Federer.

My wife Sheri Winston. This book wouldn't have seen the light of day without her presence in my life. Sheri, what a teacher you've been for me! I love you and I thank you for our life together.

And, of course, the game itself. This book is a love song to tennis.

Note to the Reader

The world would be a much kinder, gentler place if we were less blithe about blurring the boundary that separates "I believe" from "this is true." What I call conversational colonialism is one of the plagues of our minds and of our time.

This creates a problem for writers like myself who prize conciseness. One detours around conversational colonialism through regular throat- clearings: "I believe," "in my view," and so on. These are formal statements about who owns what. *This opinion is mine, the commons is owned collectively.*

These ritual repetitions clash with the virtue of brevity. If this annoys you as it does me, I request your indulgence. I seem unable *not* to clear my throat in this manner. That's how important it is for me not to commit conversational colonialism.

Yet it is also quite clear to me that some things are true, period.

The Earth revolves around the sun.
We all will die.
Getting old isn't for sissies.

Table of Contents

Acknowledgements 7

Note to the Reader 9

Table of Contents 11

Preface by Bob Litwin 15

Introduction 19

Starting Over 30

    Kingston, NY.................................. 30

Improve Your Game, Improve Your World ... 39

    A Stealth Martial Art 39

    The Quality of Attention 40

    A Resilience Intensive 42

    An Education in Time Management 44

    Dances with Boundaries 45

    The Yin and the Yang of It 47

    The Dance of Caste and Class 48

    Integrating the Two Nows 50

    A Variation on Enlightenment? 54

Spring into Action 57

    Throgs Neck, NY 57

    Roslyn Heights, NY 61

    Guilford, CT 66

    Wheeling, West Virginia 68

Tips & Tricks for Getting Better Faster 77

Know Your Learning Style 77

Images Are Everything 79

Be a Bad-Ass Iconoclast 81

Think Outside the Court 86

Know the Limits of What Your
Coach Can Teach You 89

The Power of a Simple Phrase 90

The Ascent and the Descent 91

The Geezers of Summer 97

College Park, MD 97

Kingston, NY 100

Newburgh, NY 102

Roslyn Heights, NY and Scarsdale, NY 105

Philadelphia, PA 106

Twenty Questions on the Road to Mastery .. 115

#1: What are your core issues and how do they
manifest on the tennis court? 118

#2: What negative stories arise when you
compete? 123

#3: In what ways does your personality define
your game? 125

#4: What are your most vexing
mental errors? 128

#5: What is your on-court relationship
with anger? 129

#6: What is your on-court relationship
with shame? 131

#7: How do you deal with your
     on-court failures? 132

#8: How do you deal with your
     on-court successes? 134

#9: How do you feel about competing? 136

#10: Who do you play for? 137

#11: How healthy is your relationship with the
     continuum of time? 138

#12: Are you a dancer or a dominator? 140

#13: Are you more into control or
     into freedom? 142

#14: Do you have enough li in your game? 143

#15: Where do you draw your energy and
     inspiration from? 145

#16: To what extent do the following get
     activated when you play: Beginner's Mind,
     Childish-Mind, Worried Mind? 147

#17: How loud is your Monkey-Mind? 148

#18: How good are you at practicing self-
     forgiveness on the tennis court? 150

#19: How important to you is the pursuit of
     excellence relative to the status quo? 150

#20: Are you drawn to tennis as a wisdom
     practice? 151

Fall Into Winter **153**

Longmeadow, MA 155

Torrington, CT 158

Longboat Key, FL 160

Epilogue..**175**

Preface

Bob Litwin is viewed by many as one of the best senior players of his generation. He has won 26 'gold balls' (national titles).

It takes a lot to go from ordinary to extraordinary. Not unlike Carl Frankel, I was a decent tennis player when I was younger. I started competing when I was around 28, losing regularly in open tournaments. I didn't have a dream or a plan. As George Harrison wrote, "If you don't know where you are going, any road will get you there." I thought it would be pretty easy to win tennis matches, but I quickly found out that much more was required than the basics of being a good athlete and hitting a lot of tennis balls.

At 32, I tried out for the Maccabi Games. I won a couple of matches in the pre-qualifying and headed to Philadelphia for the tryouts where I played a recent member of the Harvard team. Outmatched, I lost 6-0, 6-1. Someone who'd watched the contest asked me the score. I was shocked when they said they couldn't tell from watching who had won. It's odd how a random comment can make a big difference — Carl recounts the same experience in his book. In both our cases, it gave us clear direction — it told us where we wanted to go. In my case, that meant winning matches, winning tournaments, and a national ranking. A purpose always helps people get somewhere. Mine was extrinsic. Wins and rankings.

As Carl shares in this book, those goals are not necessarily what get you where you want to go. Also, when you get there, you may find that where you wanted to go isn't all it's cracked up to be. There may be something better at the end of the rainbow. Not unlike the protagonist in Paolo Coelho's *The Alchemist*, who discovered that the journey truly is the goal, you may discover that competition delivers life lessons that are much more important than your win-loss record.

What I came to realize — and this is what Carl expresses so clearly — is that there is a way to redefine 'winning' in tennis competition. There are more important goals out there than match and tournament success.

Years ago, I heard Billie Jean King say to a group of tennis pros, "Be sure to tell your students that it is not about the wins, it is about the journey. The ups and downs, the people you meet, the bonding, the work towards improving, and so much more."

I raised my hand and said smugly, "That is easy for you to say. You've won 39 Grand Slam titles."

She fired back, "That is why you should believe me. I've been to the top of the mountain and the trophies are scattered on the path. It is how I became who I have become that is the ultimate victory."

Carl's story attunes us to the reality that the wins and rankings are temporary, but the inner growth lasts forever.

Reading *Tennis as a Wisdom Practice* inspired me to review

why I have continued to compete for 39 years despite the fact that my tennis results have been far beyond what I ever hoped for. I was reminded that after winning the 55s World Championships, I was told by the International Tennis Federation that I would be ranked #1 in the world when the next rankings came out. My ego was through the roof. I thought I had truly arrived. Within days, though, that subsided. I felt more confused than celebratory and grew quiet when people congratulated me. How could I be the world's best when I wasn't even the best player that I could be?

Carl's book brought me to the question, "Why do I play competitive tennis?"

At the beginning, it was all about the results. When I won, though, I made excuses for my wins. The other guy didn't play well. The draw fell apart. I was lucky. And when I lost, it just felt plain awful, so either way didn't feel great.

I kept playing anyway. Over time, I came to realize that competition was helping me grow both as a player and a person. Here's some of what I learned.

How to be a good winner and a good loser.

How to develop my craft.

How to problem-solve.

How to squeeze a little more energy out of my body and my mind when I was exhausted.

How to continue to find positivity when I was on the verge of losing, sometimes to the extent that I came back and made a match of it.

How to search for the quiet within the storm, to find calm

in the midst of a self-perceived pressure moment.

How to have a purpose on each shot.

How to try to work it out when my opponent was doing all he could to keep me from working it out.

How to be fully engaged.

How to be pushed to my limit, when feeling like I just couldn't squeeze out one more drop of focus or effort and finding a little bit more.

How to have a reason that would push me to the gym, to run sprints, to do agility drills.

How to eat well, even though I would prefer to have a burger and fries.

How to discover new ways to define success.

How to love the texture of the experience.

How to redefine winning so that I could win every time on the court.

How to change counterproductive stories so that I could play unencumbered.

How to get to equanimity.

Thank you, Carl, for encouraging me to write this preface so that I could renew my connection with how much I love the ongoing work of making my time on and off the court meaningful and special.

Reader, I hope you will have as compelling an experience as I did when you read these pages. This is a rich book with material to ponder on every page.

— **Bob Litwin,** *performance coach*

Introduction

"Begin at the beginning, the King said, very gravely, and go on till you come to the end: then stop." - Lewis Carroll

It's a few years ago. I'm chatting courtside in my home town of Kingston, NY with a tennis buddy.

"I've been getting video coaching from a guy in California named Brent Abel," T.N. tells me. "He's a highly-ranked supersenior. I sent him a clip of my hitting with you and he said, 'Who's that guy you're hitting with?'"

"His name is Carl Frankel."

"How old is he?"

"I don't know. Sixty-seven? Sixty-eight?"

"Tell him not to turn seventy. He could be a top-ten player. We don't need the competition."

I was gobsmacked. I knew I was in good shape for my age and a solid 4.5-level player who might or might not be able to beat my more robust, somewhat heavier, and definitely stupider teenage self. But a national ranking wasn't something I'd aspired to since I was a highly-ranked Middle Atlantic junior whose career, such as it was, had peaked at the age of sixteen with a trip to the national juniors in Kalamazoo, solid thumpings in the first round in both singles and doubles there, and nary a hint of a national ranking. And here was that middling junior prospect, projected as top ten!

As a high school player and then in college, I perceived anyone with a national ranking as high above me on a Himalayan peak. I was far below them, nothing special, tending to my yaks.

In fairness, I was laboring for much of the time at a disadvantage. I went to Princeton at sixteen, putting me two years behind my freshman peers — and some freshman team it was. It handily beat the varsity, which won the Ivy League that year and was one of the top ten teams in the country. I was intimidated simply sharing a court with the top guy on the freshman team, a dude named Bob Goeltz who smoked like a champ, gambled like a champ, and had a backhand to die for. As early as freshman year, it was clear that I was never going to play an actual intercollegiate match, so why bother? No surprise, then, that my attention turned to the intersecting attractions of anti-war politics, the hippie spiritual revolution, and the free-love lure of getting laid.

*Princeton freshman team, Class of 1970. I'm in the back row, next to 6'8"
Heng-Pin Kiang. Henry Kennedy is in the back row next to coach John
Conroy. The fearsome Bob Goeltz is bottom row, third from left.
Those things in our hands are called wooden rackets.*

After graduating from college and law school, I taught tennis for a time in Europe and even got paid to play low-level club tennis in Austria. After that, the game became an occasional recreational activity for me. I won a Litchfield County (CT) championship when I was in my 40s, but I only played sporadically. For about fifteen years, from 2000-2015, I didn't even pick up a racket. Arthritis kept me from running two steps, much less scampering about on a tennis court. And then, in 2013, I got both knees replaced. A little over a year later, I remembered that I used to be a tennis player and picked up a racket again. And here it was, a couple of years later, and I was being told that I might soon be among the top ten nationally!

The world is full of wonders, isn't it?

At 21, a runner-up in Switzerland.

The astonishment that descended on me when I learned how Brent Abel viewed me comes with a coda. One of my regular partners (and rivals) as a Mid-Atlantic junior and then in college, where we were classmates, was a fellow named Henry Kennedy. Big smile, bigger forehand, and very much a player of my level. Out of casual curiosity, I'd checked out the national supersenior rankings shortly before my conversation with T.N., and there was my old friend Henry Kennedy, ranked at #83. I was very impressed. Had he gotten that much better? Had everyone else regressed? I didn't know, but if Henry was in the top 100 nationally, that meant I could be, too.

We scheduled a get-together and played a set and a half. It was close enough for me to think that he hadn't outpaced me completely.

Eighty-three wasn't Top Ten, though. That gap, which seemed huge to me, remained mysterious, ineffable.

This is a story, among other things, about pecking orders, about caste and class, and about an activity where caste and class are irrelevant. The pursuit of excellence. Because our gifts differ, some people achieve mastery faster than others. It's an inherently egalitarian activity, though, because it's the practice, not the outcome, that produces the most essential rewards, and the practice is available to us all without regard, as they say, to race, color, creed, or place of national origin.[*]

Any practice, including the practice of tennis, requires

---

[*] Outcomes also produce rewards, of course. Beating strong opponents and winning tournaments feels good. Victory and defeat are both imposters, as Rudyard Kipling has reminded us. Still, if I'm going to hang with imposters, I'd rather have them be smiling.

virtues like discipline, self-observation, emotional honesty, and humility. These are the skills we get better at even if we still have trouble fixing our forehand volley. When we embrace a practice, it helps us to pierce the veil of caste and class and to respect the ultimate equality of us all. Indian sadhus, beggar-monks, provide a useful model here. They've shed the trappings of caste and class and are completely dedicated to the pursuit of spiritual excellence.

Needless to say, this book wasn't written for sadhus. Sadhus can't afford a tennis racket. They're not playing our game so much as we're playing theirs. Aren't we all seeking peace of mind in a world that throws up roadblocks wherever we turn?

Over the months and years that followed Brent Abel's casual comment, I decided, what the hell, to find out if I could actually be a top ten tennis player for my age group. What had been a super-fun recreational activity became something more — the pursuit of mastery and a wisdom practice.

This is the journey I share in these pages.

I imagine us sitting around a campfire as I share my thoughts and my adventure. The engine of the story is the same as it ever was: What happened next?

Did I get that top 10 ranking? Read on and find out.

It's one thing to embark on a perhaps quixotic quest, and quite another to write a book about it. But spinning books out of my experience seems to be what I do.. A challenge or insight arises that compels my attention — I dive into the topic, learn more, and emerge with something that strikes me as useful and interesting. Then I write about it. Writing is how I learn and writing is how I share what I have learned. I share my insights not out of vanity, but in the hope that there are people out who will find them, as I do, useful and interesting.

Over two decades ago, a thought came to me in the liminal space between sleep and waking: We do three main things in life. We pursue objectives, we participate in society, and we seek meaning. This turned into a book: *Out of the Labyrinth*.

Over a decade later, my relationship was going through a rough patch. My yearning for a happier intimate life took form as a solution-oriented book: *Love and the More Perfect Union*. Our relationship is thriving now.

And then along came tennis.

See problem, engage problem, write about the damn thing.*

The decision to proceed was made easier by the fact that I was already journaling about my efforts. I had decided to record my progress, or lack thereof, years before that fateful comment by Brent Abel. Much of what I recorded was technical. To the extent that that material has value, it is only for myself and so I have left it out of this book. But there was meatier material too, some of which has made it into these pages.

My enthusiasm for the project has been tempered by doubts. Do I really want to be so public with who I am, blem-

---

* I also write more traditional books. Two books on business social and environmental responsibility, a sex-education book, and in a five-year moment of madness, an erotic novel.

ishes and all? Will people think ill of me for it? Will they see these pages as an extended exercise in self-absorption and even grandiosity? Or, less of an indictment but an indictment nonetheless, will I be charged with the misdemeanor of breaking the unwritten social rule that people, men especially, are supposed to present a strong and solid front and keep their frailties to themselves?

I decided to proceed for reasons both personal and political. I'll put aside my penchant for self-deprecation and state without adornment that I view this book as an exercise in healthy self-confidence, born of the desire to co-learn in community.

There's something else, too. To the extent that this book comes across as transgressive, I view that as entirely a good thing. I am wholly in favor of transgression so long as it is healthy, thoughtful and well-founded. A lot of our norms are more harmful than not. I firmly believe, for instance, that the world would be a better place if we abandoned our false fronts and shared the reality of our inner lives honestly and with dignity. When our issues and insecurities become a matter-of-fact and non-shameful part of what we bring to the world, we implicitly invite others to do the same. We model a more authentic and connected mode of relating.

The notion that this book may embolden people to adopt this stance is one of the reasons I'm putting it out there. Less pretense means less work for priests and therapists. That's not a bad thing.

Mardy Fish, the former US number one, would probably

agree with me. He developed an anxiety disorder so disabling that it forced him to pull out of a round of sixteen match with Roger Federer at the US Open, a match that he described as "having trained for all my life." He's gone on record that his situation was aggravated by the fact that training from an early age to be a 'tennis warrior' inculcated in him the belief that a professional athlete should never show weakness. He is convinced (and I agree with him) that hiding his condition only made it worse.

Many top players, including Serena Williams and Roger Federer, thanked him for coming out. They got it, even if society writ large doesn't. Transparency and community are healing.

There is a second and related issue. Might my openness put me at a competitive disadvantage? For years, I've worried about double-faulting at critical moments. The serve is the only stroke in tennis that we control totally. When we miss, we have only ourselves to blame — no one was hitting the ball at us. This makes it ripe territory for those who are prone, as I am, to an "I'm a choker" narrative. I went there as a young tennis player, and that Old Story, while much reduced, whispers in my ear every time I prepare for an important second serve. *The shame of losing your cool! The shame of not meeting the moment with boldness! The awful shame of not being a man!*

There: Now you know that I have a special relationship with my second serve. I imagine you across the net from me. I'm facing a match point. I've missed my first serve and I'm going through my usual routine before I hit the second. You're preparing yourself for the return and you're thinking, 'Carl has choking on his mind.' Does that give you a competitive advantage compared to your not knowing what I'm thinking?

Nope.

For one thing, we all have our ancient voices. It's not like you're picking up on an invaluable 'tell.' In the great Becker-Agassi rivalry, Andre discovered early on that he could predict where Boris was aiming by which side of his mouth he stuck his tongue out on just before he served. He never shared this publicly, saved his knowledge for critical points, and was so successful that Becker complained to his wife that Agassi "seemed to be able to read his mind." He wasn't reading his mind, though — he was reading his tongue. Now *that* was a competitive advantage. That you and I and every tennis player who has ever lived is capable of getting tight isn't the sort of knowledge that gives their opponent an edge.

Another consideration: That tiny voice has the power it does for one reason only: Because it's a closely held secret. By bringing the disinfectant of sunshine onto it, we take away its power. I'm actually helping myself by going public.

Yup, I'm human. So are you.

A key message of this book is: *Bring it.*

A few comments about the nature and structure of this undertaking may be useful. Let's start with something it is *not* — The Inner Game of Tennis, Version 2.0. I re-read Gallwey's iconic book in the run-up to writing my own, and while it has much to recommend it, it also struck me as a bit outdated and naive. Gallwey merits big kudos for breaking new ground with the important point that tennis has an inner dimension and requires more than technique. At the same time, his approach comes across as simplistic. He's basically saying, Tell your Inner Critic to fuck off, trust your inner wisdom, and you'll release the kraken of your genius and become excellent quickly.

But technique matters, too. Tennis clubs and public parks are littered with people who have never taken a lesson and are doing their own thing. You can spot them from a mile away because their technique sucks. These people will never get beyond the limbo of bad mechanics.

In hindsight, *The Inner Game* comes across like the lopsided bodybuilder who's built up his right side (the Inner Game side) while leaving his left side (good technique) alone.

We've come a long way since Gallwey shared his very useful insights into positive thinking and faith in the body's natural intelligence. We've even gotten a new profession, the sports psychologist! But let's get real here — and real means more complicated. Tennis is an integral activity. It requires a healthy marriage of mind, body, heart and soul.

This book is deeply *integral* in both form and substance.

It is integral in *form* because it combines a personal what-happens-next story with ruminations on the deep structures of the game and tips for accelerated progress.

It is integral in *substance* because it advocates for a holistic, all-parts approach to the game. I firmly believe that you'll get better at tennis (and at life) to the extent that you synergize your inner game with technique. Yes to trusting your inner philosopher and artist!

And yes to your inner engineer as well.

We are all inhabited by many selves. This book is about becoming One.

One damn good tennis player.

Starting Over

KINGSTON, NY

When you haven't hit a tennis ball for fifteen years, it feels like the very first time no matter how advanced you were. The first time I tried to hit a serve, I missed the ball completely. Once I started competing recreationally, every time an opponent threw up a lob, my notion of success was modest indeed — all I wanted to do was make contact with the ball.

One of my earliest efforts to reclaim the game took place at a lovely two-court indoor facility ten minutes' drive from my home. I came off the court and was greeted by one of the owners who said, "We went to law school together over forty years ago." James and his business partner Matt invited me to join a group of 4.0-4.5 players who mostly played doubles and with whom I quickly fit in. I was somewhere in the middle of the pack and was made to feel welcome. I soon remembered how much I loved the game and played as much as I could, which wasn't as often as I would have liked because I live in the northeastern U.S. and playing tennis indoors in the cold weather gets pricey fast. Between my regular doubles games, practice sessions limited to ball-striking, and the occasional singles match, I did manage to get on the court 8-12 hours a week. I gradually started to play better. It wasn't fast enough for me to think, I'm better now than I was last month. Year to year, though: Absolutely.

Most of my doubles pals played for the exercise, the fun, the companionship, and the occasional grand point. I wanted all that too, of course, but I also wanted to elevate my game. I wanted, so to speak, to climb the ladder. If I was a 4.5 at the ripe old age of 66, could I be, say, a 5.0 by the time I hit 70, an age that seemed inconceivable at the time (and to some extent still does)?

As the months and years passed, my pursuit of tennis mastery came to claim a disproportionate share of mind. It wasn't obsessive, but it wasn't casual either – can we agree on 'quasi-obsessive?' I regularly watched YouTube tennis videos (both the great players and the great coaches) – I journaled my ups and downs – I talked technique and strategy to any partner who didn't zone out immediately – I awoke more than once at night to a glowing insight about a nuance of stroke production.

I knew I faced multiple challenges, starting with my personal limitations. I am a good but not great athlete with ho-hum foot speed and a less than impressive first step. I was old enough to be on Medicare – and every day was making me older. While I was in a lot better shape than most sixty-somethings, my body was tight and inflexible from a lifetime of not stretching.

There were also technical limitations. Compared to your run-of-the-mill player, my form is excellent. Still, there were shortcomings. My forehand tended to be too straight-line and compact and my service toss was habitually too far left and behind me. I gripped the racket too tightly and my left arm tended to drift without structure or purpose. My right elbow tended to have a mind of its own, flying away from my body on my serve, forehand and volley.

Old habits die hard. One of the great challenges of tennis is that there is so much going on in any given stroke that it's difficult to focus on a single shortcoming over time, especially without a pro — or, even better, a pro equipped with video — to oversee your performance. I'd start a practice session resolved to work on my flying elbow on the forehand, only to discover that if I set up correctly, it didn't happen … and that required a full shoulder turn using the left arm to provide structure … and suddenly I wasn't thinking about my flying elbow, I was working on the modern unit turn.

I am a very lateral thinker who is blessed and cursed by something called ideaphoria, the capacity to have lots of ideas in a short amount of time. This, along with the inherent nature of the game, made it difficult for me to focus over time on a single liability. I kept switching partners, so to speak. Tennis-improvement polyamory!

Every tennis stroke is integral, a fully interwoven system. Maybe my flitting focus helped me address the system aspect of stroke production — maybe it slowed me down. It's beyond my ken to say.

I was facing an even bigger challenge than fine-tuning my technique. My basic style had become obsolete. When I learned to play in the mid-20th Century, wooden rackets were the order of the day. Names like 'Wilson Kramer' and 'TAD Davis' ring a nostalgia bell for me — these are the brands of my youth. In the mid-1970s, Jimmy Connors came along with the steel T-2000. Soon after, the technology dam broke and composite rackets became the tool not only *du jour*, but of the years and decades that followed. Rackets became bigger, more powerful, and also more forgiving.

What they and new string technology made possible rewrote the rules of technique. New lingo emerged: The 'unit turn' (pivoting the entire body to hit a forehand, not just the shoulders), the 'lag-and-snap' (activating the wrist separately from the rest of the arm rather than have it be a single integrated motion), and more. Entirely new stroke techniques became possible: Planting and swinging entirely off the back foot on the forehand without shifting weight to the forward foot, hitting backhands open-stanced, hitting full drive volleys instead of the usual truncated stroke, using a lariat finish on the forehand with the racket doing a flashy three-sixty over the ball-striker's head.

These same technological advances changed the practical geometry of the court for competitors who'd integrated these changes at a high level. Instead of the standard three to four feet behind the baseline, the world's best players doubled the distance and sometimes returned serve from ten feet or more behind the baseline..

Combined with scientific training techniques, the quality of world-class tennis soared. When I compare today's best players to the generation of Borg, Connors, McEnroe, and Lendl, I damn near see two different sports. Today's players are like Marvel Comics superheroes. Put, say, Federer at his peak against Borg or McEnroe at their peak and I'm convinced that Roger would win easily.

If I wanted to upgrade my game more than on the margins, I'd need to do more than fine-tune my technique; I'd have to reinvent my game. I needed to learn to make the technological marvel that is the modern tennis racket work for me. How to get better? "How do I get to Carnegie Hall?" the tourist asks the rabbi whom he encounters on the street. The perhaps-familiar answer: "Practice, practice, practice."

It was way too late for Wimbledon, but if I applied myself diligently, I could reasonably hope to become more adept.

Social 4.5-level doubles, while useful in many ways, didn't get me the reps I'd need to climb the ladder. For that, I needed a regular practice partner. I found one in Steve Macy, an artificial-intelligence brainiac who liked to hit but not play points. For the next few years, we played weekly, often multiple times. We drilled: Ten approach shots, extended crosscourt-to-crosscourt, extended down-the-line to down-the-line.

Then another practice partner came along. For decades, Rich Rumble had been the head pro at the Bonnie Briar country club in Westchester County. During that time, he'd been recruited to hit with Ivan Lendl, who lived up the road a piece in southern Connecticut. That's how good a ballstroker he was – and remained, despite physical nicks that cost him a few steps of quickness. We both liked nothing more than to go out and, for lack of a better term, 'feel like a tennis player.' He hit a Goldilocks ball that wasn't too fast or too slow, and delightful to practice against. We'd hit for an hour or an hour and a half and virtually without exception leave feeling gratified at what felt like a great mix of focus and fun.

Since Rich was also a professional tennis teacher (he continued to freelance part-time), I also had the benefit of the occasional insightful suggestion. I will never again hit a forehand volley without Rich's ongoing coaching ("Keep the racket head above your wrist! Keep the elbow tucked into your side!") running like a chyron through my mind.

I was aided and abetted in my practice by the occasional toke of marijuana which, far from distracting me or causing me to subside into gales of giggles, helped me stay focused while also delivering the occasional insight of real value. For instance, I tend to be an arm player who doesn't engage his hips and core enough. The explanation goes beyond the wooden rackets I grew up with. When I first picked up a racket at the age of seven, my main — and, really, only — challenge was to make contact with the ball. I did so by bringing my awareness into my shoulder, which I then used as my fulcrum for making contact – and there it had remained, creating a sort of dismal separation between my right arm and hand, whose job it was to hit the ball, and the rest of my body, which except for the running part was mostly along for the ride.

This insight came into port on the steamship Demon Weed.

I played very few tournaments, and enjoyed minor local success when I did. With county election official Tom Turco, I won the 45-and-over county doubles championships. Two years later, I came within two points of winning the doubles championship at the Woodstock Open, a similar local competition with stiffer competition because it was open to all ages. My partner Joe Luzzi and I won the first set and got up by 5-4 in the second, my serve. I double-faulted twice and we went on to lose the set and match. But I digress into therapy territory.

A supersenior version of myself teamed up with Joe Luzzi against Ahmed Mansour and Mitch Adler before the finals of the 2020 Woodstock Open.

Roughly midway between the re-launch of my love affair with tennis and my launching myself like a projectile into the world of USTA-sanctioned tournaments, supersenior guru Brent Abel made his offhand comment about my being a top ten candidate if I were to play in the 70s division. The seed he'd planted sprouted a few years later. I liked where my game was headed, and I liked what it did to my head. You only live once.

I decided to go for it.

I joined the USTA and perused the supersenior tournament schedule. There were surprisingly few opportunities, attrition and indifference combining to reduce demand. One tournament caught my eye, though: The National Indoors, scheduled for Houston in March 2020. I'd been playing indoors almost exclusively since my return, had gotten used to playing in perfect conditions, and was put off by the variability of outdoor play. The high sky threw off my timing on everything overhead — the sun was the occasional blinding impediment — the wind had been created by God solely to mess with my timing.

I also was uncomfortable playing on clay. I'd been playing on a hard Deco-Turf surface and found the bounce on Har-Tru to be unpredictable and generally annoying. The National Indoors would be played on hard courts. It seemed like the perfect venue for me to launch my new quasi-career on the supersenior circuit – and I'd have six months to get ready for it.

As I started preparing in earnest for my new deadline, I was put in mind of Samuel Johnson's famous maxim: "When a man knows he is to be hanged, it concentrates the mind wonderfully." I was about to play a national tournament and found myself practicing more intently. Unlike the person facing the gallows, though, I found the experience exhilarating.

I prepared with focus but not full-time. My off-court training was minimal. I viewed my challenge as one of tennis execution, not health and fitness. I couldn't remember the last time I'd played tennis and gotten tired. I'd also managed to stay remarkably injury-free since my return. Although my frame was tight and inflexible, it didn't seem to matter —and hitting tennis balls was a lot more fun than stretching and lifting weights. In retrospect, the mix was wrong. My preparation was semi-serious.

It turned out not to matter. As I was preparing to play in Houston, Covid was heading to our shore. In March 2020, the tournament and the pandemic collided in real time. A week before the tournament, I canceled my flight. A few days later, the tournament was called off.

At the time, I was disappointed. I was pretty sure my game had gotten better and I hoped to surprise some people. In hindsight, I'm glad the tournament was canceled. Match toughness comes with experience, and I had neither. More than a year was to pass before I played in my first USTA-sanctioned tournament. During that time, despite the challenges of Covid and the ravages of entropy, my game actually got better. I'd still be coming in green, but this time I'd start sensibly. I'd find my footing by playing lesser local tournaments. Better that than making my first tournament a national gathering with geriatric studs flying in from all over.

As John Lennon famously put it, "Life is what happens when you're making plans."

My tennis career in the 70's division would have to wait until I was 71.

Improve Your Game, Improve Your World

The United States Tennis Association (USTA) has an aggressive youth outreach program with a special focus on communities of color. Seen cynically, this is simply good business. They are mining for talent and they are mining for revenue. But they have a real social purpose, too. Tennis mirrors life. The kids think they're running around having fun when in fact they are learning character traits that will serve them in all facets of their life.

When I make the point that tennis skills are life skills, I'm invariably met with a knowing head-bob. Tennis as a school of life is a truism as well as true. Never has anyone followed up with what seems like a useful and obvious question: *In what ways?* That is the subject of this chapter.

A STEALTH MARTIAL ART

The martial arts are "codified systems and traditions of combat," according to our friends at Wikipedia. The combat giveaway is in the name: Martial as in Mars, the Roman god of aggression and war.

The martial arts are also, as per about a million pop films, more than that. They are practiced for reasons of "physical, mental and spiritual development." (Thanks again, Wikipedia.) And so we have Bruce Lee, and the Shaolin temple, and Zatoichi the sighted swordsman who kills the bad guys as a blind man because it's more artful that way.

The dojo is a sacred place. But you already knew that, grasshopper.

When you sign up for the martial arts, you're registering for a course in character development. As you climb the belt-color ladder, you become more disciplined, more courageous, more focused and present, and more finely balanced emotionally and energetically.

(Or so the story has it.)

The martial arts, in short, train you to be better at life. This is part of their mystique. Of their brand.

The story of tennis is different. It's seen as a strictly secular activity, a world away from Eastern mysticism. It's people chasing a ball, people chasing victories and – at the rarefied top – people chasing big prize money.

The sport can be as fertile a spiritual learning ground as the martial arts. It may not come to us on a platter labeled 'Wisdom Practice,' but that's what it is if you choose to see it that way.

We need a new story about tennis.

THE QUALITY OF ATTENTION

The First Commandment of tennis is, "Watch the ball."

This guidance is as essential as it is basic. Its value is also somewhat limited. It's pretty vague — it invites the question:

Watch the ball in what ways?

- There's noting the rotation pattern of the ball.

- There's focusing on the outside edge of the ball.

- There's watching the ball with your feet, by which I mean imagining it's your feet doing the watching, not your eyes, so there's a more direct link between watching and moving and you get off the mark more quickly.

- There's seeing *only* the ball.

- There's seeing the ball as the central object in a larger context, like when you're returning serve and trying to read pace and direction from the service action while also watching the ball, or hitting a ground stroke while playing doubles and trying to sense where your opponents are positioned.

And this is just for starters.

Many years ago, I learned a form of meditation called Dharana. You focus on a single object, your breath or a sound or object. If it's a physical thing, you look at it. That's all you do. You look at it. You give yourself permission to get still, and you invite yourself to notice. You relax into the particulars.

Dharana teaches a crucial life skill. People learn to focus, deeply and intentionally. I can't imagine a more important spiritual training — it's the quality and direction of your attention, after all, that determines the quality and direction of your life. If you've developed the ability to attend at will to *this*, but not *that*, you're like a god compared to most of us. You've learned to control your inner weather.

Watching the ball can be a single-focus meditation. You do it by trying to track it with a soft focus, an activated body, and an alert mind. You do your best to return to that awareness every time the ball comes at you. That's hundreds or thousands of times over the course of a single session.

If you wish, you can add experiments run on different particularities. What happens when I watch the ball *this* way? What happens when I watch it *that* way? This is how we get better at tennis, by ourselves asking this sort of question.

Meanwhile, in parallel, we're being trained in perhaps the most important life skill of all. We're learning how to upgrade the quality of our attention.

A RESILIENCE INTENSIVE

Life comes with a guarantee. Bad things will happen to you. And then, if you do get off the mat, bad things will happen again.

Resilience, bounceback-ability, is right up there with attention management as one of our most important life skills.

For all their importance, what I think of as our soul muscles are barely on the cultural radar. We're not taught resilience, certainly, not unless we join the Marines. I never gave thought to the importance of resilience until midlife. That's on me to some extent, and it's also on our culture.

The tennis court is a great place to develop your resilience. Roger Federer once noted that the best players in the world usually don't win more than 52% of the points in a match. When you win 60%, it's a spanking. Let's say a match has 100 points. Even when you're winning easily, you're being handed forty chances to practice resilience. And what about those easy putaways you dumped into the net? When the disappointment is stronger, you get to practice resilience squared, and you get to do it again and again. Even the Federers of the world make unforced errors twenty, thirty, forty times per match.

Every time you swing at the ball, you're looking at an imminent opportunity to practice resilience. Is it better to make than to miss, better to succeed than to fail? Of course it is, but failure – no, failures! – are guaranteed. And failure is a learning opportunity.

I'd rather succeed than fail on the court, every shot, every point, every time. But downs come with ups in the game of life, and failure has its consolations. Its arrows point us toward playing better, and it also gives us the opportunity to exercise that all-important soul muscle, resilience, over and over again.

The three-time Grand Slam winner Stan Wawrinka has a tattoo on his left wrist. It's a Samuel Beckett quote and an ode to resilience: "Ever tried. Ever failed. No matter. Try Again. Fail again. Fail better."

AN EDUCATION IN TIME MANAGEMENT

If you're like me, you can get disregardful – wasteful, even – in your relationship with time, the most precious commodity we have. Our world feeds the impulse with drugs literal (drugs you smoke, drugs you pop, drugs you shoot) and figurative (the Interwebs, television, shopping). When we go down these paths, we fall prey to the mythical seductress Circe out of Greek mythology who turned sailors into swine. We become disconnected, oblivious, unaware.

Every moment is precious on the tennis court, too, and not only because our time is limited there, as it is in life. We improve faster and compete better if we stay fully present to every possible moment.

Between shots during a point, do you pause to assess your last shot rather than hustle directly into position for the next?

Between points, do you plan consciously for the next round of action or do you wait more passively than not for it to reveal itself to you?

Do you get distracted by negative stories ("I'm too slow," "my opponent's too good," etc.) that take you into the Eternal Now of negative thinking ("always," "never," etc.)?

These are bad habits because they're *inefficient*. You develop mastery on the tennis court, and also in the court of life, by making the most of every moment.

DANCES WITH BOUNDARIES

We live in a world of boundaries. Between the roadway and the sidewalk, there's the curb. For every 'this' and 'that,' there's a dividing line between. Where does a shrub stop and a bush begin? One might even say, hehe, that boundaries rule.

Many of our boundaries are social, not physical or linguistic. Let's say a stranger approaches you. The rules of civility require them to keep a certain distance. If they get too close, it tells you they're threatening you or coming on sexually or just acting clueless and weird. Unless we're totally lacking in social intelligence, we know when that line has been crossed. We're mammals, and mammals are territorial.

You can't have a rule without boundaries. Whether you're not saying "thank you" to someone who's just passed the salt, or breaking and entering a house at midnight, you're crossing a line.

Boundaries are bound up in our inner rule systems, too. Hold 'em or fold 'em? Turn the other cheek, or deliver the comeuppance they so richly deserve? Every decision has one or more boundaries built into it.

When I was coming of age during the Great Hippie Bubble, there was a widespread assumption among the psychedelically enlightened that behind the veil, we were all One, and that boundaries were an illusion and a spiritual obstacle. There was genuine insight in this, and they were also wildly wrong. The experience of mystical unity is a real one. At a more mundane level, though, we're separate. This is where boundaries rule.

Boundaries rule on the tennis court, too. This goes way beyond the obvious in/out nature of each shot. Suppressing negative thoughts is a key component of match toughness. Who enforces it? The border police.

There's also the higher-level challenge of maintaining the right balance between emotion and analysis, between hot and cool. I watch Rafael Nadal with awe because he plays every moment as if it were his last without ever sacrificing strategic clarity. When you let your passions get the better of you (or, more accurately, the worse of you), they create a single wash of emotion that makes it more challenging to think with precision and to execute skillfully. Emotions are *chi*, pure energy. Boundaries are *li*, structure, the walls we build to channel and direct our *chi*. On the tennis court, you want to be left-brained as well as right-brained, *li* as well as *chi*, poised as well as passionate. You want to ride the boundary between them.

Boundaries are also implicated in individual strategies. *Don't hit a drop shot if you're standing on the baseline.* I transgress this rule so often that a friend calls it a feature of my game, not a bug. I usually do it for a bad reason. An upwelling of doubt about my next groundstroke, or maybe the rally's been going on a while and I'm getting bored. Sometimes I do it for an okay reason. I'm up 40-love in a tight match and I want to throw a scare into my opponent. I'm crushing my opponent and allowing myself, this one time, to go for the thrill of a show-off shot because you're also playing to have fun, right?

"There are games beyond the games," Stringer Bell tells

Avon Barksdale in *The Wire*. Well, there are also rules beyond the rules, in tennis as well as in life – and every damn one of them has boundaries.

When you're in a backcourt rally, when do you focus on keeping the ball in play and when do you go for an outright winner? If you were to unpack the variables that go into the decision, you'd probably come up with answers like the nature of your opponent's shot, the extent to which you're in a good position, and your confidence level about going big. The decision has to be made on the fly, though, holistically, through a sort of animal knowing, your body speaking tennis wisdom to you. Clear, simple rules win tennis matches — you don't want to overthink things. And that calls for intuitive, well-honed boundary management.

THE YIN AND THE YANG OF IT

In the Taoist tradition, the universe is powered by equal energies, *yang* and *yin*. *Yang* is focused, directed, forward-moving. *Yin* is receptive and embracing. They are complementary: Sun and moon, act and be, penetrate and receive. Masculine and feminine, as per the ancient tradition.*

It serves us to be able to access whichever energy is most appropriate for a given situation. Let's take the familiar situation where Jill shares an unhappy work situation with her husband. He has basically two options: He can listen empa-

---

* It's important to note the difference between masculine/feminine and male/female. This discussion is about energy, not anatomy. Not all women are 'feminine' and not all men are 'masculine.'

thetically, or he can make suggestions. It's a familiar female lament that guys try to fix things when all the woman wants is to be heard. They tend to be action-oriented when she wants him to be receptive. A great response from hubby would be, "Would you like me to just listen, or would you like me to offer suggestions?" In other words, "Would you like me to be more *yin* or *yang*?" Because there might be times when she actually wants him to fix it.

Both *yin* and *yang* play important roles on the tennis court. The return of serve provides an excellent example. As my opponent is going through his preparation routine, I give myself two instructions: Get still and then react quickly. This is strong *yin* making way for strong *yang*.

Serving provides another example. You get power on your serve from an explosion of kinetic energy that you direct up and at the ball. It's not a purely *yang* activity, though. Usually, there's also a moment of stillness. Typically it comes when the ball has been tossed into the air, the tossing arm is still extended, and the body is poised for the strike. For a fraction of a second, you become more like a statue than not. That tossing arm is like a mast on a ship, still and steadfast in the wind — your kinetic chain, unleashed, is like a wave washing over it.

Yin and *yang* are complementary. We learn to invoke them as needed as we get better at tennis.

THE DANCE OF CASTE AND CLASS

I happen to be one of those people who historically has

felt intimidated by people who nominally rank above me. There are two reasons for this: I had a semi-famous father, and I also went through elementary and high school two years younger than my classmates. Both are prescriptions for imposter syndrome and concomitant feelings of not rating, which I've spent five decades shedding.

I'm not alone in my susceptibility to dominance hierarchies. Many, if not most, of us are susceptible to feeling inferior to people who are above us on the totem pole, whether that be because they're one of the cool kids or have a national ranking or celebrity status.

One of our essential tasks in this lifetime, it seems to me, is to shuck off the filter of caste and class and to see ourselves and others as equally important beings regardless of our places on the pecking order. When Jesus said, "The meek shall inherit the Earth," I believe that's what he meant, although "the egalitarians shall inherit the Earth" would have framed it more precisely.

(Last I looked, of course, Jesus didn't speak great English.)

Tennis provides a spectacular opportunity to shed our caste-and-class filter. In my first year playing supersenior tournaments, I spent a fair amount of time checking out where my opponents were on the ranking table. If the guy was ranked twentieth, I figured I'd have a problem. If they were in the hundreds or unranked, they'd be easy pickings. That's not how it always turned out, though. More than once, I cruised past the highly-ranked guy and met my match in the 'lesser' player.

To some extent, this is because the supersenior ranking

system is flawed. You get participation points for playing in tournaments, and some tournaments have tiny draws because the pool of players at 70+ is smaller than for younger cohorts. But it's also because the underlying mindset – *fear those high on the totem pole* – is a slave mentality and the opposite of useful.

Roger Federer, who is a font of wisdom as well as genius, once said, "I respect everyone and fear no one." He plays the person, not the shell of status that surrounds them. It's an iconoclastic attitude, one that goes against the grain of our social training. It's a fundamentally more logical approach, though, than the shock-and-awe approach to social status that our culture inculcates in us. Celebrities are stand-ins for the Olympian gods our culture tries its best to do without. That's why our hearts go thump when we're introduced to them.

On the tennis court, we play one point at a time, one game at a time – and one person at a time. A person with a beating heart and with strengths and weaknesses, just like us. We thrive to the extent that we can engage our opponent on this basis rather than through the scrim of a fiction that declares our relative status – higher or lower, better or worse – to the world.

INTEGRATING THE TWO NOWS

Imagine a continuum bounded by what I think of as the "two Nows."

The Immediate Now, and the Eternal Now.

Let's say you're walking down a street and someone comes at you with a knife. Your pupils dilate and the adrenaline kicks in. Everything about you is focused on survival. You are fully consumed by the 'Immediate Now.'

At the other end of the continuum is the 'Eternal Now.' An appalling detail from my personal life: In 1979, two career robbers broke into my parents' home and murdered them as they slept. I learned about their murder in the early evening, was kept busy by the police until the early morning, and went to bed around 2:00 AM. I barely slept and woke up as dawn was breaking. The leaves on the tree immediately outside the window were blowing lightly. A flock of birds was swooping and swirling in the sky above. It was about 6:00 in the morning, but chronological time as we usually experience it had stopped existing. The tree outside my window was all trees throughout all time — its leaves were all leaves throughout all time — the birds in the sky had been soaring there throughout all time. Shock had taken me out of my body and into forever. I was inhabiting the Eternal Now.

In *Lapis Lazuli*, the poet W.B. Yeats writes about the Eternal Now. He imagines two old men high on a mountaintop looking down on the full pageant of life.

> *... (A)nd I*
> *Delight to imagine them seated there;*
> *There, on the mountain and the sky,*
> *On all the tragic scene they stare.*
> *One asks for mournful melodies;*
> *Accomplished fingers begin to play.*

Their eyes mid many wrinkles, their eyes,
Their ancient, glittering eyes, are gay.

We spend our lives traveling between the two Nows. For some people, their default habitat is up the mountain, above the storm and fury of everyday reality. For others, their natural habitat is in the valley. Philosophical traditions are made of this. If you're a romantic, you embrace the passions of the Immediate Now. More classically-inclined people see things from more of a witness perspective and are predisposed to focus on higher-level patterns and principles.

Tribal rivalries are made of this, too. If you're an alpine sort, you might be inclined to view valley-dwellers as 'drama queens.' And they, in turn, might dismiss you as 'not in touch with your emotions.'

As I've grown older, I've come to believe that healthy aging takes us up the ladder of abstraction away from passionate engagement and toward the infinite and more distant and eternal. There's a logical and ultimately healthy reason for this. The body knows what the heart resists. One of the tasks of old age is preparing to die. We do so by heading up the mountain. Passion isn't for the old. It's for people who are procreating, for people who are politicking, for people whose world it is now.

Let's apply this to tennis. Competitive sports perform an important social function. They provide a largely or completely safe outlet for aggression. When we compete on the tennis court, we're inhabiting an archetype that's been with us since humanity's first days. *War! Combat!* Although I'm not actually at risk of getting hauled off the court in a body bag, competitive sports produce the same fight-or-flight impulses as actual do-or-die situations. Tennis drags you into the Immediate Now.

We compete well to the extent that we resist getting completely sucked up by the Immediate Now. We fail at this when we lose our sense of context. Every point in a tennis match is nested inside a game, which is nested inside a set, which is nested inside a match, which is nested inside many matches, which is nested inside life itself. The more we can maintain this sense of context while in the heat of battle, the less likely we'll be to fret over losing a single point or game. We're less likely to worry about 'dying,' so to speak, because we know that we'll be reborn in the next game, in the next set, in the next match. Context, which is to say the bearing in mind of the full continuum of time, is like Delilah taking her scissors to the hair of the Immediate Now's Samson. The quicksand of excessive urgency becomes a meadow we can frolic on.

More times than I care to count, I've mapped out a plan for a match and totally forgotten about it in the heat of battle. It's very difficult not to get lost inside the adrenalized do-or-die moment. Fear of failure, fear of 'dying,' fixes a person's attention on the immediate essentials – hitting the ball, making smart tactical choices, practicing resilience. One's eyes are fixed on the battlefield — one loses sight of the stars overhead.

When you can remember your game plan, that's a sign that you're still up the mountain.

When the coach of the promising American player Seb

Korda says, "You don't open the microwave until the timer goes off," he's talking about keeping one's eyes up the mountain. Don't worry about single games or even single matches. Climb up out of the Immediate Now. Keep your eye on the longer term. Or, as he puts it, "trust the process."

When Roger Federer said "It's only tennis" after losing the 2019 Wimbledon final to Novak Djokovic despite holding two match points on his own serve, he was sharing his sense of context, his view from up the mountain. Wise words indeed. (But having twenty Grand Slam trophies on your shelf may make it easier to be philosophical.)

Maintaining a healthy perspective in the heat of life's challenges is a daunting challenge. Tennis helps us learn how to do it.

A VARIATION ON ENLIGHTENMENT?

Every tennis player aspires to be 'in the zone.' During these rare and exalted moments, excellent performance seems to flow forth effortlessly without extraneous thoughts or fear. We experience ourselves as beyond our normal flawed selves. It feels borderline miraculous.

There's a story about the legendary actor Laurence Olivier that may actually be true. He'd just finished playing Hamlet in the most brilliant performance of his career. A friend came into his dressing room to find that the Great One had trashed it completely.

"What the hell?" his friend said. "You just had the greatest performance of your life!"

"That's right," Olivier raged. "And I don't know how I did it."

Thus the glory, thus the challenge, of being in the zone.

What does the experience of enlightenment feel like? Damned if I know, but I'll hazard a guess. Everything flows easily, naturally, effortlessly. It is a place of peace, of acceptance, of deep and abiding equanimity, where one easily inhabits one's best and wisest self and the extraneous noise is dialed down to zero. Bad outcomes are promptly let go of — ditto for good outcomes, too. Full flow state becomes the norm.

I'm treading in uncertain waters here, a situation that encourages questions more than answers. So I will leave you with this. *Is being 'in the zone' a secular experience of enlightenment? Do saints and gurus live 'in the zone?'*

I can't help but wonder if the pursuit of the zone in tennis, which is something every serious tennis player yearns for, is actually the pursuit of enlightenment, draped in sweaty secular clothes.

Might being 'in the zone' be a marker, a sign on the Enlightenment Highway reading 'Head this way?'

Spring into Action

THROGS NECK, NY

"They sure threw you into the deep end of the pond," Mitch Adler said. "You're up against a legend."

I'd just told him who I'd be playing in my first USTA tournament, a mid-April 65-and-over tournament because why not? I had the weekend free and was eager to test myself against supersenior competition although it was an age group down from the 70s division.

My first-round opponent was someone named Steve Gottlieb. This was what had prompted my friend's response – Mitch had spent years in the tennis industry and knew the Who's Who of the supersenior world.

The name also rang a bell for me — it conjured up the image of a slender leftie with a big serve-and-volley game. I had no idea why I was making that association, but there it was.

The tournament was being held on indoor Har-Tru inside a tired bubble in the shadow of the Throgs Neck Bridge.

Steve emerged from the locker room wearing a USTA national team warm-up. I didn't take it amiss, preferring Muhammad Ali's view of things: "If it's true, it ain't braggin.'"

The match was over quickly. His game was the same one I thought I remembered, albeit not quite as intimidating. He missed his first three serves, which briefly gave me hope, then he locked into gear and gave me a healthy drubbing. It was competitive for a few games, then he switched into overdrive and dominated. His side-to-side movement wasn't great, but he approached and covered the net superbly. I never found my timing – this was my first time on clay in six months, and I'd never hit a ball at this facility – and I was on my heels throughout. The 6-1, 6-1 final score was a fair reflection of how the match had gone. A whuppin' is a whuppin'.

Which Muhammad Ali didn't say, but might have.

We were gathering our belongings and chatting courtside post-match when it all came back to me.

I'm fifteen years old and sitting on a grassy hillside at the Hackley School in the New York City suburb of Tarrytown. I'm there to watch a tennis match. My personal hero Dick Stockton, who is a year younger than I, is playing the number one guy on the Columbia freshman team. A few years earlier, Tennis Magazine had called Stockton the "best player pound-for-pound in the world." He was a true phenom, the Rafael Nadal or Carlos Alcaraz of his time. He'd drubbed me 6-1, 6-2 at the Orange Bowl in Coral Gables, FL a few months earlier. It hadn't occurred to me that I might actually win — I felt honored just to be out on the court with him. Stockton would go on to make the global top ten and the semi-finals at Wimbledon – the guy could flat-out play. Presumably the Hackley coach had set up the match with Columbia because they needed to find competition for Dick. The likes of myself, attending a private day school just across the

Hudson, wouldn't provide enough challenge. His op-
ponent had been, that's right, Steve Gottlieb, the very
same lefty who'd just whupped me. It had been quite
the jaw-dropping experience for me — Gottlieb had
beaten my idol handily in two straightforward sets.

I told him the story and he remembered the match, too –
my memory hadn't failed me. We started chatting and discovered that we had a fair amount in common beyond our love of
tennis. We'd both gone to Ivy League schools but had chosen
a more creative and financially less remunerative path than the
silver-spoon one that had been laid out for us. Photographer
for Steve, writer for me. Quality of life over amassing wealth
– that had been the ticket for us both.

I went home and googled Steve Gottlieb. His status was
merited. Four-time All-Ivy while at Columbia, member of the
District of Columbia Jewish Athletes Hall of Fame (yes, there
is such a thing!), winner of multiple 'gold balls' (national supersenior titles).

I'd been thrown into the deep end, indeed.

It turned out that we lived an hour and a half away from
each other. A month later, we got together for a social game
and lunch midway between our two homes, and he became a
font of advice for me. A mentor, really, as I took my first baby
steps on the supersenior circuit.

He told me to expect a considerably lower level of competition in the 70s than in the 65s.

He told me that I needed to develop match toughness,

and the only way to do that was by playing so many matches that "no one match mattered that much any more."

He told me that if I were to play Bob Litwin, the reigning Big Dog of the 70s division, I'd "have a chance on my best day to beat him on his worst day."* Not exactly encouraging words, but honest well-intentioned feedback is good feedback, and that was what this was.

I knew exactly what Steve meant. Once you've played enough tennis, it's easy to size up the competition. Some people will never beat you — some people you'll never beat — some will be a contest every time — and then there are those below you who have a shot, even if only remote, at beating you, as well as those above you who you could beat, but not often. Steve's observation put me in mind of Vitas Gerulaitis, who famously said at his post-match press conference when he beat Jimmy Connors after sixteen consecutive losses: "No one beats Vitas Gerulaitis seventeen times in a row."

I was to Bob Litwin as Vitas was to Connors. Without the losses yet, but that was another — and perhaps future — story.

Needless to say, I didn't want to be looking that far uphill at anyone. Had Steve failed to appreciate my true genius on the tennis court? Much as I wanted that to be the case, I had to admit – probably not. A man of his experience would have had me pegged within the first three minutes of our warm-up.

Well, then, might I be able to play catch-up? Maybe,

---

* Litwin wasn't ranked #1, but that's only because rankings reflect how much you play along with how well you do. He'd earned his reputation over the years with — as of now — 26 national senior titles.

just maybe, I could improve enough so I'd have more than a puncher's shot at beating people like Litwin — and Steve Gottlieb.

This, too, seemed unlikely, given my age and good but not great athletic ability. A man could dream, though. Could I achieve the improbable? This seemed like a reasonable aspiration, not because I'd probably make it – a person had to be realistic – but because of how much fun it would be to try. How can an old man – or anyone, for that matter – get better faster? It seemed like a great next chapter for my life.

ROSLYN HEIGHTS, NY

My first 70's singles competition came about three weeks later. The venue was a six-court Har-Tru facility at a club called The Tennis King in the Long Island village of Roslyn Heights, NY, not far from where Bob Litwin had grown up. One parked at the base of a small rise tucked away behind the town hall, walked the thirty yards or so to the crest and there were the courts, two rows of three aligned behind each other.

I'd drawn the first seed, which didn't surprise me. It was a small draw, with only two rounds before the finals, and I was exactly the sort of unknown who'd be slotted against the guy who, coming in, was deemed best in show. In this case, his name was Alec Roberts. The name meant nothing to me, and I chose not to research his tennis bona fides. If he was the first seed, that was good – or bad – enough for me.

Our warmup gave me a modicum of hope. He wasn't

a classic ball-striker — I thought I spotted some technical glitches that I might be able to exploit. The match started, and something unexpected happened — I won the first set handily. Six-love! I didn't play great. I just tried to keep the ball in play, and he obliged me by missing frequently. In retrospect, I think there were two reasons for this. He was rusty – this was his first tournament of the year – and he might also have been taken aback, and ultimately put off his game, by the fact that the nonentity he'd drawn in the first round had what Brent Abel and Mitch Adler had called a top-10 game.

At this point, I had my first of what would prove to be many sobering encounters with the perils of match inexperience. I figured I had the match in the bag and got careless. Meanwhile Alec changed his strategy, mixing the occasional serve-and-volley with a newly lethal drop shot. When he won his first game, I thought to myself: That's the last game for him! But the shots he'd missed in the first set were going in now. Twenty minutes later the second set was over. He'd won it 6-2.

The finale would be a ten-point pro tiebreaker. As we sat on the sidelines before the finale, I was feeling cranky. I didn't like how I'd competed, and I didn't like how I'd played. I'd driven over two hours to play in the event, and for what? I wasn't even having fun. Did I really want to travel close to five hours for this one or two more times? In the heat of the moment, it seemed like a bad idea. I made a decision: If I got to match point, I'd retire and hand him the win. I could do better with my time.

The tiebreak started and I got an early lead. As my play – and with it my hopes – picked up, I decided I'd been a damn fool to think about quitting. I'd stay the course, win or lose, and compete for the entire tournament.

Tiebreaks are crapshoots by definition. A couple of good shots here, a couple of errors there. I pulled this one out by 10-5. When his final shot sailed wide, I heaved a sigh of relief. Silly me, to have considered retiring!

When the match was over, we got to talking. Alec was an interesting guy — I liked him immediately. He'd been a broadcast journalist — now he was in the admirable business of building homeless shelters, including several in the mid-Hudson Valley where I lived. I told him about my dark night of the soul as we prepared for the concluding tiebreak.

"I'm glad you decided to continue," he said. "You have too much game to walk away from supersenior tennis. Did you know that you just beat the ninth-ranked guy in the country?"

I blinked. "Wow, really?"

This news put a fresh spin on everything. If I could beat the number nine player on a nothing-special day for me, maybe what Brent Abel had said was correct and I could be among the best in the 70s division.

My semi-final opponent was a man named Henry Steinglass. The tournament director authorized us to play at his home club in Westchester County, which was an easier drive for us both. The surface was red clay. I never felt seriously threatened and won 6-2, 6-3. He played the soon-to-be-familiar-to-me supersenior game of standing a foot inside the baseline and using that forward positioning to throw in the occasional well-disguised drop shot. He couldn't quite keep pace, though. When it was over, he said simply, "You have too much game for me."

We got to talking. It turned out that he was 78 years old. Seventy-eight! I was deeply impressed by his fitness and competitive pluck; he was one of those guys who could beat me on – Gottlieb's notion – my best day and his worst. He was still practicing law, but his main job consisted of caring for his wife, who had dementia. Henry was low-key and soft-spoken, but as I got to know him better, I came to admire him increasingly for what I came to see as his unassuming heroism.

The finals were up next. I'd seen my opponent play and knew I'd be in for a tussle. Michael Harvey could still move pretty well, and he had the groundstrokes of a teaching pro, which he'd been for much of his life. This time, I researched his background. He was ranked #11 nationally and had played multiple close matches with Alec Roberts.

The first set wasn't close. He won it 6-2. At no point did I feel overmatched, but the points kept going his way. The second set went my way by an identical score. The differences were miniscule – a few more errors by him, a few less by me. As the games fell my way, my confidence grew and his seemed to get some cracks in it – maybe it was occurring to him that he might lose.

The momentum shifted in my direction. On one point, I chased down a drop shot, froze him with a fake down the line, and slid it cross-court for a winner. On another, he hit a very high lob from well off court. I put it away crisply and efficiently from just behind the service line, displaying a confidence in my overhead that is usually reserved for indoors. He grimaced and shook his head both times — this told me I was getting to him. Deep into the set, he tossed his racket against the fence, silently but with palpable frustration. All this was very gratifying.

The pro-tiebreaker final set was another crapshoot. I won it by 10-5, happily accepted a Tennis King tee-shirt as my prize, and headed home. I called my wife with the happy news – *I'd just won my first 70s tournament!* – and followed it up with a call to my friend Doug Grunther, whom I've known for over 20 years. We have a deep historical connection — he is all of six days younger than me, and my father, a philosophy professor, had been his favorite teacher at Columbia, where he'd played #1 on the tennis team.

He congratulated me on my victory and we started reminiscing. "There was this guy named Michael Apfelbaum," he said. "He played at Columbia for a year and then dropped out, I'm not sure why."

I recognized the name. "Mike Apfelbaum? I played him when I was 14 or 15! It was the semi-finals of a tournament in northern New Jersey. He was ranked in the top ten nationally in the 14-and-unders. I really wanted to beat him. It would have been a real feather in the cap for me. I lost 9-7, 7-5 and I had set points on him on the first." I paused. "Funny how we remember all the details from 55 years ago, isn't it?"

I could sense his silent agreement on the far end of the

line. Then he said, "I believe he changed his name to Michael Harvey."

"Michael Harvey??? That's the name of the guy I just played!"

"Well," Doug Grunther said, "you just played Mike Apfelbaum."

So there it was. In my first USTA-sanctioned match, I'd played a guy, Steve Gottlieb, whose image was emblazoned in my mind because he'd handed a can of whup-ass to my tennis idol. In my fourth USTA-sanctioned match, I'd won a grudge match against a guy who'd beaten me fifty-seven years prior, and I'd done it without even knowing it was a grudge match!

I wasn't playing supersenior tennis.

I was starring in *Back to the Future*.

GUILFORD, CT

June brought me to the Guilford Racquet Club for a regional Category 3 tournament. This was one level up from the tournament I'd just won and put it in, or at the very least on the fringe of, the category of 'major event that players travel a distance for.' In this instance, that prominence was mostly theoretical. The draw was barely larger than the one at The Tennis King.

Again, I was unseeded.

My first round was an uneventful 6-1, 6-0 victory. I wasn't thrilled at how I played. My opponent had no firepower, but I'd been unable to finish points as quickly and efficiently as

I wanted to, especially since these were hard courts, where it should have been easier for me to hit through him.

Not that it mattered – I was on to the next round.

Gary Chafetz is an ex-journalist of some renown. It took me a bit of time to figure him out. He has an unconventional game with lots of slices and chops — he'd hit some ridiculously good shots and then miss a bunch. After the first few games, I decided it could go either way, but then the points and games started piling up in my favor. It was a hot day, and the reflection off the hard surface made it hotter. Gary draped his head in ice packs when we changed sides. The final score of 6-1, 6-2 belied the fact that we'd been out there close to two hours.

I was into the finals of this humble Category 3 tournament.

My opponent would be the winner of a match between Jon Wilson and Lloyd Clareman. Jon had solid strokes but seemed a bit slow afoot. Lloyd was more of a free swinger whose shots were going in that day. Either one of them could beat me, but I didn't feel intimidated.

I ended up playing Clareman. The match was never close. The shots he'd made the day before were landing out now. I was probably getting to more balls than Wilson had, and this may have frustrated him and caused him to overhit. Whatever the reason, I soon had another 6-1, 6-2 victory, this time with less sweat involved.

I'd won a prestigious Category 3 tournament with the loss of only seven games. I liked how this sounded, especially when you ignored the fact that Guilford had been a Cat 4 sheep in

Cat 3 wolf's clothing.

"You lost seven games in the entire tournament?" Steve Gottlieb said when I checked in. "You have a future in the 70s."

WHEELING, WEST VIRGINIA

I was feeling elated by how things had gone so far. I'd played two 70-division tournaments, one of them a Cat 3, and I'd won them both. Along the way, I'd beaten guys ranked ninth and eleventh in the country. I didn't have a ranking yet, but I was on my way.

Someone pointed me to a website, supersenior.info, that listed all the winners of geezer Category 3 tournaments. I was on the list. So was someone named Gary Jenkins, who'd claimed all the other 2021 Cat 3 titles. This was impressive and just a bit intimidating, especially when I researched his record and discovered that he appeared not to have lost more than three games in a single set. How would I do against him? Not well, I had to assume.

An opportunity to find out lay just around the corner at the Cat 3 Jack Dorsey Memorial Tournament in Wheeling, West Virginia, where Jenkins was registered to play. My wife and I decided to make the trip, which was a full day's drive away — Covid ruled out flying. We were drawn not only by my pursuit of a national ranking, but because according to my friend Henry Kennedy, it was a lovely venue and well worth the visit.

He was right. The Oglebay Resort is an impressive example of how a public-private partnership can benefit the public. It features a large lodge, multiple golf courses laid out over hundreds of acres, a full-size swimming pool, and eight Har-Tru courts laid out on two levels of hilly terrain. Deer were everywhere.

Most of the names in the draw meant nothing to me. Gary Jenkins was playing; I'd get to check him out. So was a guy named John Tashiro, who had a high national ranking in the 50s division. I'd met him at Guilford, where I'd been impressed by the immense solidity of his game — he'd primarily played in Japan and been a highly ranked junior and college player. Like me, John was interested in socially responsible business — we hit it off immediately. Henry Kennedy was there too, he of the big smile and flashy cars (he'd showed up for our reunion match driving a yellow Ferrari). I was still very much a newbie, but I was starting to get the rhythm of these events, the overarching good will and the easy collegiality–and I was also starting to see familiar faces.

There were also faces that should have been familiar, but weren't. On my first day at the tournament, I watched a fellow named Francis Kreysa play a match. We were subsequently introduced and he said, "When I was growing up, there was a kid named Rook Frankel who did well in the Mid-Atlantic division. Any relation?"

"That was me," I answered, laughing. "'Rook' was my nickname back then."

I was still in *Back to the Future*.

My first-round opponent was one Dennis Posteraro. I re-searched him and found that he was ranked in the middle 100s. I knew enough by now to attribute no significance to this.

"You're playing Denny?" Henry Kennedy said when I told him. "He's a very good player." An expression of alarm must have crossed my face, because he followed this up with, "It's not that you can't beat him. You're a good player, too. After all, you beat Michael Harvey." Another pause came. Then: "One place he has an edge is match experience."

That again.

Denny proved to be solid, indefatigable, and fleet of foot for a guy in his 70s. It was an interesting match. Not only was I up against a stalwart opponent, but it also amounted to my unofficial introduction to the broader community. My game, my deportment, my general character. A couple of dozen peo-ple watched and, I assumed, took notes, if only informally.

I didn't play badly. "You had Denny on a string through-out the match," Erin Geraci, the genial and extroverted wife of tour regular and retired Pentagon lifer Allen Geraci told me. She was right — I was on the front foot throughout. It didn't help, though. I lost 6-4, 6-2, done in by a combination of Denny's compete level, my inability to adjust strategically to his refusal to submit, and my fragile second serve, which flipped me the bird with both hands, and then mooned me, in the second set.

I did have my moments, though. A pattern emerged early on. We'd rally, I'd hit a drive into his forehand corner, follow it up to the net, and he'd pass me with a sharp crosscourt. Once, when the same pattern unfolded, I moved to my right, only to have him hit the ball, this one time, behind me. I had only one choice – play the shot from behind my back. I stuck my racket out and made contact on the half-volley. It landed two feet across the net, bit and took a 90-degree spin to the right for an unplayable winner.

Denny had chased my shot up to the net. As I handed him a ball for his next serve, I said, "That was on purpose. Can I quit now?" He smiled, said nothing, and went back to the business of beating me.

The second set was never in serious doubt.

When the match was over, Dennis, who's a very nice guy, said: "I really had fun playing against you. You're a strong player. You have a strong forehand." (He paused for thought.) "And a good backhand down the line." And then came the clincher. "Welcome to this community. It'll be great to have you be part of it."

His words took much of the sting out of my loss.

When the draw is big enough (and sometimes when it's not), tournament directors hold a feed-in consolation so that players won't have made the trip for just one match. This would be my destiny. I won my first match handily against a retired pilot named Joe Touzin. We played at a secondary venue away from Oglebay Resort on a bone-dry court. I played pretty well and Joe, who had an attacking game that could have given me a lot of trouble, made it easy for me. "I can play a lot better than that," he said when it was over. I believed him.

I told Joe that this was my first year playing the supersenior circuit and that I was hoping for a national ranking. "You'll get there," he said. "Just keep playing tournaments."

My next match took place the following day on a back court at the more congenial main venue. My opponent was a big left-hander named Gary Weinstein who proved to be another one of those players who lacked the consistency and speed to pose a serious threat. I won 6-1, 6-0, losing one less game than I had against Touzin.

My opponent in the consolation finals was an ophthalmologist from Ohio named Phil Roholt. He came onto the court with his face slathered in zinc and draped in protective clothing head to toe. Arms covered, legs covered, big floppy hat – all I could see of him was his face. It looked like I was playing a ghost.

Based on my assessment of him during the warmup, I figured I should beat him easily. His forehand seemed iffy and his power modest. At first, things went according to plan. I won the first set 6-0. The score didn't seem flukish — if I simply kept on keeping on, I'd walk away with the kissing-your-sister thrill of having won the consolation.

At which point, the roof fell in. Phil took off his zinc along with his extra layers of clothing, pitting me against an actual human, not a ghoul, and he revised his strategy as well. These goddamn guys who don't know enough to quit while they're behind! He started pushing – hitting balls soft and deep, one after the other – and mixing this up with sneak attacks, rushing up to the net while I was focused on one of his bloops and even throwing in the occasional serve-and-volley. Before I knew it, he'd jumped to a three-love lead. I battled back, but my confidence was now in the rear-view mirror. Phil was playing a different guy from the one who'd begun the match, someone who was scared to miss, scared of losing, and generally roiling in self-loathing.

When the racket strikes the ball, it is the tennis equivalent of where the rubber meets the road. Its success is determined by many factors, including technique, energy, and attitude. Failure feeds failure in this moment — success feeds on success. Roholt's tactical adjustment had toggled me into negativity. My shots emerged from a morass of doubt and frustration. One consequence: My technique failed me. I stopped shifting my weight, including on my serve, which is a recipe for double faults. When I tried to hit out, I did so without structure and flailed more than swung with predictable results.

People were watching. I'd made a positive impression against Denny Posteraro. Now I was making a negative one. Knowing this only made me unhappier.

In quantum mechanics, there's something called Heisenberg's Uncertainty Principle. It's become popularized to mean this: At any given moment, a quantum object has the potential to be either a wave or a particle. The observer can't know which it will be, ergo 'Heisenberg's Uncertainty Principle.' Well, allow me to introduce Frankel's Uncertainty Principle:

Whenever the racket meets the ball, the strike can be fueled by either confidence or doubt.

Some axiomatic truths flow from this:

- Unsuccessful shots fuel doubt, successful ones fuel confidence.

- People perform worse from the 'doubt zone' and better from the 'confidence zone.'

- Transient doubt can harden into negative expectations, i.e. an internal narrative that views failure as the norm. Transient success can harden into positive expectations, a narrative where success becomes the norm.

- This process is one of the main explanations for the mysterious but real phenomenon known as momentum.

My match with Phil Roholt provided a great example of this. He started making shots, I started missing shots, and as things cascaded I was thrown back to my time as a junior tennis player when I lost to more than one pusher and walked off the court feeling more ashamed than my soul could bear. My second set in the consolation finals returned me, one dismal point at a time, to that adolescent and despairing mindset.

I wasn't fifteen, though. I was seventy-one, hopefully with more perspective on my situation than I'd had back then. Point by point, I battled back without ever reclaiming my game (or pride). I even went ahead by 6-5. Ever the optimist, I decided that the close 7-5 final score would be offset by the fact that I'd won in straight sets. But then Phil won the next game and the second-set tiebreaker by a very close 7-5. It would come down to a third-set pro tiebreaker.

Somehow I prevailed. The final score was 6-0, 6-7, 10-5.

Joe Touzin had been watching the match. I walked up to him, feeling more like I was slinking than striding.

"You looked like a different player out there," he said. "Everything off the back foot."

"At least I won," I consoled myself with.

I could feel myself blushing.

Joe Touzin then gave me a gift that I remember to this day. "It happens to all of us," he said.

Gary Jenkins won the tournament, defeating Allen Geraci handily in the finals. I saw enough of the match to get a sense of Gary's game. I didn't feel intimidated by what I saw. If he was better than me – and based on his record, he probably was – it was because his game was like mine, only a bit more solid across the board.

My wife and I took a leisurely two days to drive home, stopping along the way at a lovely 18th Century inn to pick up some bedbug stowaways, who decided that my wife was tasty, but not I. As we drove through the peaceful Pennsylvania countryside, with days until her suffering began in earnest, I had ample time to meditate on my uneven performance. I decided that I was learning some hard lessons.

I needed to get better at overcoming self-doubt and hanging in there in the face of my opponent's stubborn and irrational refusal to yield.

I needed to get better at responding to mid-match adjustments.

I needed to get better at maintaining a decent standard of play no matter what my opponent threw at me.

I needed to stop playing to impress people.

I needed to compete for the pleasure of competing.

I needed to take the shame out of my game.

Steve Gottlieb had talked about the power of match experience. So had Henry Kennedy. I was beginning to understand what they'd meant.

Tips & Tricks for Getting Better Faster

KNOW YOUR LEARNING STYLE

If you want to get better fast, it helps to know what teaching styles click for you, and which don't. Some tennis teachers can't help you because they don't know what they're doing. Others are unable to do so because their teaching style, which is also typically their learning style, isn't a good fit for you. You can still get a lot of value from these mismatches, but you'll usually do better with a teacher whose learning style matches yours.

The Harvard professor Howard Gardner has identified eight types of intelligence: Visual-spatial, linguistic-verbal, interpersonal, intrapersonal, logical-mathematical, musical, bodily-kinesthetic, and naturalistic (an odd category that seems to mean, roughly, 'drawn to nature').*

Looking at the Gardner list, I see myself as ranking high in three areas (linguistic-verbal, interpersonal, intrapersonal) and mediocre or worse in the other categories. The theory of multiple intelligences can be humbling for people like myself who've always been good book-learners.

Now let's turn to tennis-teaching styles. Over the course of the 2021 season, I was helped by two teaching pros. Mark

---

* I'm convinced there are more, but that's another story, if not another book.

Santucci was captain of his Division 1 college team and is a solid 5.5 player who really knows the game. One of the things he worked on was helping me modernize my forehand. At one point, he advised, "Imagine yourself aiming your left elbow at the target as you go into your backswing and having your right elbow aiming at the target when you're done."

This image clicked for me immediately. Mark had given me a mental representation that I could easily visualize and work with. If I did what he said, I'd have no choice but to engage my hips, back and shoulders — I'd be hitting a modern forehand.

It wasn't transformative because a mental representation is only useful if you actually remember and apply it. Forgetfulness is the price I pay for having an agile mind; I often move onto the next thing without a trace of memory of what I've left behind — thanks a bunch, attention-deficit disorder! But when I do remember to dredge up Mark's image, it is immediately useful.

I've also worked with my friend Rich Rumble, a teaching professional with beautiful old-style strokes and, like Mark, a deep understanding of the game. Rich has an exquisite volley, which he developed as a nationally-ranked junior table tennis player. I have an, uh, less-than-exquisite volley — it tends to be insufficiently compact and a bit too wristy. With Rich's help, I've gotten better at keeping the racket head above my wrist and my elbow into my body rather than leaving it to flap around outside the frame of the stroke structure.

"Like this," Rich will say, and then he shows me the short

chopping motion he wants me to imitate.

His teaching style — *look and imitate!* — arises out of his learning style, which flows directly from the fact that he has a high 'BK-IQ' — Bodily-Kinesthetic Intelligence Quotient. Because my highest intelligence is linguistic-verbal, it's not as easy for me to play monkey-see, monkey-do as it is for people whose brains are wired like Rich's. Because of my learning style, it would be easier for me to develop a Rumble-esque volley if he were to lob a mental representation my way, for instance by saying, "Imagine that you're giving somebody a rabbit punch."

This is absolutely not a criticism of my friend Rich Rumble. He's a great coach and my game has gotten better with his help. And: You'll get better at tennis faster if you work with someone whose teaching style matches how you learn.

IMAGES ARE EVERYTHING

No matter what type of intelligence we lead with, we develop excellence through a process of triangulation. Our mind forms an image of what we're supposed to do, and we try to imitate it with our body. It's an activity with three participants — operating system manager, mental image, physical action.

See the image in your head, instruct it to happen with your body.

This is how we develop mastery, with compelling mental representations that we mimic endlessly.

There are physical representations: *Swing your back foot to the front when you hit your forehand.*

There are 'role-model representations': *Set up for the over-head like Roger Federer.*

There are dream-like representations like the one that occurred to me recently: *Play from high on the ziggurat.*

This last example could probably use some unpacking. It came to me during a ten-minute spell during a practice session when I felt completely in the zone. During that time, I had the distinct sense that I was executing at an entirely new level of performance. It all came together; I felt relaxed, loose-wristed, quick-footed by my geriatric standard, and plugged in.

That's when the image of the ziggurat occurred to me — ziggurat as in stepped pyramid.

The image felt meaningful to me, which told me that it had come to me from the unconscious, which is also the source of our dreams. A plausible interpretation arrived swiftly. With its many terraced levels, the ziggurat symbolized the ascent to mastery. In the image (essentially, a single-frame dream), I was standing on one of the uppermost terraces. The ziggurat signified my place in the hierarchy — specifically, how far I'd climbed. It was advising me of my status — it was telling me where I fit in.

Keeping the image in mind helped me maintain my flow-state level. Just as the American flag is a simplified stand-in for the complex of emotions we call patriotism, the ziggurat was a stand-in for the complex of emotions that had me performing in the zone. If I'd tried to keep executing at a high level by constantly reminding myself to do all the technical things that were bringing me success — *Stay loose! Maintain a low ceiling! Don't be afraid to miss! Strike decisively and with commitment!* — my performance would have imploded under the weight of all those word-messages. The ziggurat image folded all that complexity into a single visual and tied it off with a self-esteem ribbon that boosted my confidence and made it easier for me to maintain my level.

Pay attention to images whether they come from someone else or from your own unconscious mind. Respect the role they play in your quest for excellence. They are invaluable.

BE A BAD-ASS ICONOCLAST

We humans are creatures of habit. We develop customary ways of doing things, and then we do them without thinking. We brush our teeth twice a day, not once or thrice. We squeeze the toothpaste from the bottom of the tube. When we play tennis, we start off by going to the backcourt and whacking the ball at the person across the net. Habits are choices that are hibernating.

Examining both your behavioral and psychological frameworks can provide unexpected insights and make you a better player. Here are five examples.

Easy Listening Tennis

Depending on who's counting, we have five or seven senses: Sight, sound, hearing, touch, and taste plus two late additions, body awareness (proprioception) and movement and balance (vestibular).

Tennis is a sight-centric game. "Watch the ball!' is the first thing our teachers tell us. That's the sense we prioritize when we step onto the court. It's a sensible habit.

It's also worth experimenting with. During a hitting session with my friend Steve Macy, I decided to focus on hearing the ball hit the racket rather than seeing it. I continued to watch the ball, of course, but in the context of a new instruction set: I was to judge my shot based on how it sounded, not on what I saw or on where it went.

I started hitting better immediately. Focusing on listening caused me to keep my head more still as I was swinging, and it also meant a momentary pause post-contact while I made meaning out of the sound I'd just heard. Focusing on listening immediately made me more chill and more still.

I told Steve what I'd just experienced and invited him to try it, too. He had the same experience.

Thus was born what I now call Easy Listening Tennis. It's a great way to calibrate your game.

Hard, Harder, Hardest

After a hitting session with the longtime teaching professional Mitch Adler, he invited me to try something. He dropped balls for me to hit with the instruction, "Swing as hard as you can."

Other than this session, I can probably count on the fingers of both hands the number of times I've hit a groundstroke as hard as possible. There's always been an intervening consideration: *Get the damn ball in!* During my time in the Adler barrel, my balls went everywhere. Into the net, to the wall on the fly, and on the rare occasion, in. None of that mattered. The entire point of the exercise, I soon realized, was to get me to throw away my prior notion of how hard I was 'allowed' to swing. The sky — or, more precisely, the field beyond the fence — was the limit.

I left the session with a fresh understanding of how arbitrary the upper limit was that I'd placed on my power game. An entirely new approach to the game had been handed to me: Instead of aiming for control and building up power, aim for power and build up control.

It wasn't transformative because old habits die hard. But it contained a sort of awakening.

Roscoe Tanner Teaches the Serve

I learned how to serve the same way most people do. I threw the ball into the air and tried to hit it with the racket. Eventually I figured out how to do that and my practicing became more nuanced.

Roscoe Tanner, one of the top players of the 1970s whose serve topped out at a near-record 153 MPH, teaches serving differently. He tells his students to find a low-hanging branch on a tree that is at the exact height where they want to be striking the ball, and then to practice hitting the branch until they have a deep embodied understanding of this ideal point of contact.

Next up: Perfecting the toss. Get a bucket, place it on the ground at the base of the ball's ideal trajectory, then practice the toss until it goes in the bucket every time.

Last of all comes putting the two together. Toss to the bucket and swing at the branch, timing the swing so the ball will be struck as it passes through the strike zone.

Tanner teaches his students to aim at a spot, not the ball. Like swinging as hard as possible and prioritizing hearing over seeing, it breaks the frame of our usual process. If the quality of his serve is any indication, it is also mighty effective.

Right Is Wrong. Good Is Bad

It's not only your habitual ways of doing things that benefit from fresh scrutiny. There's also how you judge your performance, for instance, how you differentiate good from bad, right from wrong.

Our brain sends wrong messages when we're trying to get better. Because the old way is familiar, we tend to see it as right, correct. Because the new way is unfamiliar, we tend to see it as weird, off, wrong. This makes us cautious to a fault. Although we're actively trying to get better, we tend to trust our internal guidance system ("Wrong! Stop!") too much and to therefore cling to the status quo.

Dare to feel weird. It will help you get better at tennis.

The Moral/Physical Divide

For years, I had trouble telling if a ball hit to my backhand side would land inside the court or wide. I can't count the number of times I was sure a ball was headed out only to have it land well inside the line. Whenever this happened, I'd berate myself internally. *"Lazy! Lazy! Run for the ball."*

Recently it occurred to me that my failing might be physical, not moral. Maybe my eyes were processing the ball's trajectory wrong. Maybe I wasn't being a lazy good-for-nothing — maybe I was actually seeing the ball as headed out until it was too late.

I took this hypothesis to a local Feldenkreis bodyworker who looked me up and down, poked and prodded me impressively, and then sent me on my way. The result? I started seeing out balls out and in balls in. The session had corrected my vision. The only reason this problem went away was because I challenged my assumption that it was due to a character flaw.

You may be wondering why these experiments are icono-clastic, as the header of this section proposes. Unusual — yes. Innovative? That, too, maybe. But iconoclastic?

Yes.

Etymologically, 'iconoclast' means "breaker and destroyer of images." Usually, that's understood to mean statues of idols, of false gods — both religious and social — but it also has a deeper and more pervasive meaning. Norms are the 'thou shalt' and 'thou shalt not' mental structures that provide the guard rails for our daily choices. When you start examining these patterns with a view toward possibly breaking them, you are being an iconoclast.

The five examples in this section are iconoclastic in that they all tear down the 'idol' of hibernating habits. They are calls to aliveness, to fresh thinking.

Bring the invisible ink to life.

Be a conscious iconoclast.

THINK OUTSIDE THE COURT

You don't have to spend time on the tennis court to get better at tennis. In fact, your improvement can be accelerated by spending conscious time off-court working on your game. One reason for this is that when we're on the tennis court, our Prime Directive tends to be on hitting the ball inside the lines. That can be a distraction if you want to get better.

The gym can be a big part of your off-court regime. Chasing balls for hours on the tennis court will do wonders for your conditioning, but it won't address all your fitness issues. You build up muscle strength by lifting weights. You develop flexibility by stretching.

There are also off-court learning modalities that have nothing to do with the gym. I've learned an amazing amount from watching studs like Roger Federer, Marin Cilic and Matteo Berrettini:

- You may not know that Fed aims his racket at the back fence before he brings the racket up into striking position. You certainly don't know that when I tried to do the same thing, my serve improved immediately.

- Cilic's serve provides an elegant case study in how to create space between your body and your striking arm, and in how to wield the racket like a bullwhip.

- When he's changing sides during a match, Berrettini doesn't walk from his courtside seat to his place in the backcourt — he skips. He always does this. It's not a quirk; it's an instruction. He does it because a coach or trainer told him: *This is how you get your body going*. The only reason I don't do this is because it seems pretentious at my age. If I were more sensible, I'd be like Matteo.

I've also gotten enormous value from watching instructional videos. Patrick Mouratouglu, who's been in the corner of innumerable stars, offers great tips in pithy, actionable phrases: *Keep a low ceiling when you play.*

There are other great teachers on the Internet, too. *When you serve, let your wrist be like a hosecock that you've opened.* This bit of great guidance came to me from the interwebs, and it's stayed with me since I first heard it.

You can be a bad-ass iconoclast off-court as well as on. During Covid, many online tennis instructors started sharing off-court drills — shadow-swinging, footwork drills, etc. Watching one of these, it occurred to me that there was a future for an off-court practice that married tennis with *tai chi* — call it *tennis tai chi.* I envisioned it as laid out in a standardized, transmissible form, like other martial arts — start with the forehand, proceed to the backhand, then go to the volley, and so on, all performed in super-slow motion.

The benefits of *tennis tai chi* would extend to both the *tai chi* and tennis sides of the fence. Practitioners would get martial-art benefits by practicing the form. They would get tennis benefits by executing the strokes correctly without having to worry about details like timing the strike and hitting the ball in. It would be an exercise in art for art's sake, in form for form's sake, and in tennis executed for the health and beauty of the strokes themselves.

As far as I know, *tennis tai chi* exists nowhere but in my mind. It is an idea waiting to become a business (not mine!) as well as an idea waiting to be picked up and developed by individual tennis players who think it might be fun and also — *who knows?* — make them better.

KNOW THE LIMITS OF WHAT YOUR COACH CAN TEACH YOU

A good coach is a great thing to have. They can identify obvious weaknesses, suggest alternatives, and do their best to drill them into you. But you can also over-rely on them.

I've had some great doctors in my time. That doesn't mean they always had good advice for me. As laypeople, we may not have the credentials to be our Primary Care Physician, but we can and should be our Primary Care Person. Our doctors are best seen as consultants, not commanders.

The same is true for our tennis 'doctors.' Think of it this way: A medical doctor is a person with a body of knowledge and credentials that allow them to order blood work and other tests. Your standard tennis teacher is a person with a body of knowledge who may or may not be credentialed and who has zero capacity to order tests for the simple reason that the tests don't exist. A tennis pro is like a doctor who diagnoses based on walking around you from a distance. There's no prodding or palpating, and no data to refer to.

This is why their recommendations should be taken with a grain of salt. Their capacity to diagnose is limited.

Technology will soon be changing how tennis is taught. A new AI app called SwingVision provides reams of data about miles per hour, topspin rates, etc. In a few years' time, most savvy tennis professionals will probably have incorporated SwingVision or similar metrics-producing technologies into how they teach. They'll be closer to working like doctors.

In the meantime, when your pro checks out your grip and says it looks just fine, bear in mind that they don't know what happens to that grip when you're actually swinging. You may be adjusting it imperceptibly at the very last moment; you may be squeezing down too tight.

Just as we can't solely rely on others to keep us healthy, we can't solely rely on others to make us better tennis players. We have to be our own best analyst and advocate.

THE POWER OF A SIMPLE PHRASE

I'm big on affirmations, phrases we say privately to shift our mindset in a positive direction. They are like slugging a shot of self-worth caffeine: They tilt the scale toward the person and player I aspire to be and occasionally am.

Lately, I've been working with this affirmation: *There are no 'uh-oh's' in your game.*

You may find its origin story useful as you contemplate the role of affirmations in your tennis life. I was waiting to receive serve and a thought, perhaps familiar to you, flitted across my mind: *I hope he doesn't serve to my backhand.*

I've had that thought about a million times. This time, though, it was accompanied by an insight: How much I was sabotaging myself. If the server targeted my backhand, they'd confirm my fear and I'd return anxiously, with predictable results. My opponent would take note, rinse and repeat, and there I'd be, playing from a hole that I'd dug for myself.

Every time I had that thought, I was feeding a yummy

morsel into a negative feedback loop. This had to stop. But how? I decided on an affirmation that would override my sense of vulnerability. The first one that occurred to me was: *There are no weaknesses in your game.*

Not bad, but it didn't feel quite right, too intellectual and conceptual. It was addressing my head and not my gut, where the anxiety lives. And so I changed it: *There are no 'uh-oh's' in your game.*

'Uh-oh': That's the sound of anxiety when you're trapped on the tracks and the train is hurtling down on you.

The affirmation chilled me out and quickly made me a better player. I felt more balanced, even-keeled, and ready to respond similarly no matter which side the serve came to. Prayer — *please, Lord, may he serve to my forehand!* — abandoned my preparation.

Affirmations rarely are forever. Usually, they work for a while and then lose their juice. Our psyches are shaded beyond our capacity to imagine. As we move through time, imperceptibly subtle shifts happen, and sometimes they transform yesterday's "Wowee!" into today's "Wha-?"

Flip your anxieties into positives with affirmations that emerge from your soul.

THE ASCENT AND THE DESCENT

In an earlier chapter, I discussed the continuum of time that's bounded by the Immediate Now at one end and the Eternal Now at the other. This is one example of a mental conceptual ladder that goes from specifics to generalities, from less inclusive to more inclusive, from micro to macro — and back down again. We ascend toward the inclusive, and we descend into the particulars. We do this with time. We do this with just about everything.

Both the up and down trajectories play crucial roles in the pursuit of mastery. Let's consider them in turn, starting with the ascent.

We organize the world into nested boxes: A fits inside B, which fits inside C, and so on. Thus, each tennis stroke inhabits its own silo (or box, or mental category — call it what you will) within the larger category 'tennis.' The basic strokes are serve, volley, overhead, forehand and backhand. We learn to play the game by proceeding from box to box. We learn the forehand, then we learn the backhand, and progress from there to the volley, the serve, and the overhead.

This produces a predictable if not inevitable outcome: We use the same framework to analyze our strengths and weaknesses. *What am I doing wrong on the forehand? Am I making a big enough shoulder turn on my backhand?* And so on.

There's nothing inherently wrong with this approach. It's helped a gazillion aspiring tennis players over the years. It comes with a shortcoming, though — it boxes us in taxonomically at the level of *stroke categories.* What if we were to tear down those walls and adopt a cross-category lens instead of focusing on just the forehand, just the backhand, just the serve, just the whatever? What, in other words, if we were to be more holistic in our pursuit of error detection and correction?

Our medical culture provides a handy analogy. It focuses on specialization: We have podiatrists, ophthalmologists, cardiologists, and so on. In reaction, a fundamentally different approach to the practice of medicine has arisen. Integrative medicine starts off by focusing on the body as a single system and analyzes weaknesses in the various subsystems in the context of the higher-level organism that is the entire body-mind.

I'm suggesting a similar approach here. Start with the entire system and problem-solve horizontally. Both our good and bad habits tend to bleed outside their individual buckets. For instance, I tend not to give myself enough space on the forehand and to hit it from too close to my body. Well, surprise, surprise: I have the same flaw on my serve. It is a bit too compressed, unliberated if you will, and this keeps it from being as free-flowing, accurate and powerful as it might be.

What are your horizontal challenges? What would it take to address them? If you have a bad habit on your [plug in the stroke], you probably have it elsewhere, too.

Now let's turn from the ascending to the trajectory's other — and equal, not better — half: Descending into particulars.

The term comes to us courtesy of the Jesuits, who embrace context-based decision-making while rejecting the upward journey to universal principles. Known as casuistry, which has gotten an undeserved bad name, their approach dives into the details to determine the best approach in a given situation.

The world of words illuminates, and it is also a veil. Someone says something, we assume we know what they mean, and then we go off and do something based on that assumption only to learn that woops — we'd read the word tea leaves wrong. I've done this countless times. You probably have, too.

When Mark Santucci, a 5.5 player and insightful coach, told me to "Go up and get the ball" on my serve, I found it immediately illuminating. I crossed the gap that separates my mind from his intention and interpreted his words thusly: "Throw your entire body up toward the ball, and have your arm fully extended at impact."

When I tried to do as he suggested — or, more exactly, when I tried to do what I believed he was suggesting — I could sense a modest improvement, but nothing close to what I was hoping for.

And so I descended into particularities. I asked myself: "When Mark tells me to 'go up and get it,' what does he actually mean?"

As soon as I asked myself the question, it occurred to me that he himself might not know. I mean no slight by this. What "go up and get it" means when applied to me might be very different from what it means for another person, based on our relative muscle strength, flexibility, natural throwing motion, and much else. Just as we all have different fingerprints, we all have different best ways to "go up and get it."

The next time I worked on my serve, I honed in on my mechanics and emerged with a new understanding of what "go up and get it!" meant for me. I discovered that if I activated my trapezius muscles so my arm felt a couple inches more elevated than in habitual mode, that enabled me to make contact with the ball at a higher point than before. And this, in turn, made it more powerful and accurate.

If Mark had said, "Focus on your trapezius muscles — use them to raise the strike position of your racket by what feels like two to three inches," he would have descended into particulars in a manner that left me less white space to fill in. It would have been a more customized and therefore more actionable suggestion. This wasn't possible for a very simple reason — it's his body he lives inside, not mine. Mark's words had been illuminating, and they'd also been a veil in the sense that they opened the door for me to head down a wrong path.

What does 'watch the ball' mean? What part of the ball? And for how long?

What does 'continental grip' mean? Where do the fingers sit? What about the fatty part of the palm?

Questions like these are invitations to descend into particulars. We accelerate our progress when we do that regularly. The same holds true when we climb the ladder and identify flawed meta-patterns.

Ascend toward the general.

Descend into particulars.

The Geezers of Summer

COLLEGE PARK, MD

One good thing had come out of the Jack Dorsey Memorial – my first national ranking. When the next rankings came out in the middle of the next week, there I was at #24. It was a gratifying moment – and I still had the better part of the season to achieve my top-ten aspirations.

I decided to chase more points in metro DC. There was a Category 4 tournament in College Park that looked like easy pickings. There were only six people in the draw, only one of whose names I recognized: Allen Geraci, whom I'd gotten friendly with in Wheeling. I was the top seed and he was seeded second. I'd be playing someone named Jack Ambrose in the first round. If I beat him, I'd be in the finals and my ranking, win or lose, would climb into the teens.

What I had in mind didn't feel completely legitimate. I'd be working the system – 'juking the stats,' I'd heard it called. If I made it into the top 10, it would come with an asterisk. But I would still be in the top ten.

My first match would be on a Saturday. I traveled to College Park on Thursday, got settled into an Airbnb, and met up with Allen the next day for a game of social doubles. When we were done, I offered that I hoped we'd get to play each other in the finals. Allen made a little face. "Jack Ambrose is good," he said.

And he was. We played on indoor Har-Tru at the Junior Champions Tennis Center, a busy, sizable and well-maintained complex with both indoor and outdoor courts. Jack was tall and lanky. He moved well, hit his ball flat, and placed it well. It was clear from the first minute of warm-up that I'd be in for a tough match. Unlike many of the players I bumped up against, he had no obvious weaknesses.

For one set, I was in the zone. The vacuum of Frankel's Uncertainty Principle filled with the helium of confidence. I went for more ambitious shots because I believed I could make them – and I did! It was over quickly at 6-1.

My new friend John Tashiro, who was there to play in the 50s division, had been courtside watching the set — we'd warmed up together before the match. As I left for a bio break, he said, "It's inspiring watching people your age play and move as well as you do."

I felt flattered and honored. I'd played great, and now I'd gotten this wonderful feedback from a guy whose game and character I'd come to respect. Now I just had to keep going.

It didn't happen. He won the second set as easily as I'd won the first. I went off the boil and his game went up a notch. He won the important points; I started feeling like I was looking uphill. The final set score was 6-2.

Towards the end of the set, I decided to play not to win the set, but to be in a good groove for the third set pro-tiebreaker that was looking increasingly likely to decide the match. It didn't help. I never got my game back and he continued to roll.

The final score was 1-6, 6-2, 10-2.[*]

So much for juking the stats.

I now had the option of playing in the consolations (yes, in a tournament with a draw of six!). Initially I said yes. My first opponent would be someone Ambrose had beaten love and love; my second opponent would be someone Geraci had beaten love and love. Playing the consolations would be an easy way to amass more points. As the afternoon wore on, though, I started reconsidering. I'd probably already gotten a bunch of points just for getting to the semi-finals, although I'd done so without playing a match – talk about juking the stats! Consolation points in a tournament with a main draw of six would probably be miniscule. I'd play two matches, and my personal over/under would be if I lost a single game.

Most of all, I was feeling cranky. This was yet another in an expanding series of matches where I'd performed well at first but couldn't stay the course. Some of these matches I'd managed to scrape out. Not this one, though. I wanted to go home and lick my wounds.

I told the tournament director of my decision. She'd already lined up my opponent for later that day. Now she'd have to call him back and say, "Only kidding." I regretted inconveniencing her, but I stayed with my decision to practice self-care.

Only when I got home did I review the ratings table and find out that I'd gotten virtually no points out of the main

---

[*] Ambrose beat Allen Geraci by an almost identical score in the finals the next day: 3-6, 6-2, 11-9.

draw and that I would have boosted my ranking a fair amount if I'd hung around for the consolations.

I was glad to be home anyway.

KINGSTON, NY

A fun opportunity awaited me at the public courts a mile from my home – the Ulster County Championships. It wouldn't garner me ranking points, but I'd be among friends – and the commute was fabulous. I'd entered the 45-and-over singles, leaving the open division to Mark Santucci and another 5.5 stud who would eventually battle it out in a superbly contested final. I quite liked the prospect of winning a tournament that was open to players as much as twenty-six years younger than I — and I thought I had a shot at doing it.

I came into the tournament resolved to see progress at being match-tough. For me, that meant shutting the door to the past and the future, and it also meant visualizing myself inside a shiny silver vault that was a sort of psychic clean room with nary a speck of self-doubt. A match-tough player did their job — they stayed cool, calm and focused — wavering was out of the question.

Match toughness meant engaging this amateur activity in the mode of a full professional.

I won my first two matches easily. Neither posed a real test. My semi-final match did, though. My opponent was Vic Ricci, a pro at a nearby tennis club. Vic is one of those guys who gets everything back. He won't overpower you, but his game can annoy you into submission. He also throws in a left-handed serve from time to time to keep his opponent off-balance. No one looks forward to playing Vic. I won the match with the loss of only one game, but it wasn't the rout that suggests. We were on the court for a solid two hours. It was a sweatfest. He had about ten game points along the way and cashed in on only one of them.

I'd liked to have dominated as much as the score suggested, but otherwise I was happy. When you have ten game points against you and you only lose one of them, you're either damn lucky or doing something right. I gave myself points for match toughness.

The finals were against a friend named Rich Juman. He'd played a lot as a young guy. He understands the game and has good strokes and a memorably understated style. He never looks like he's straining, and every once in a while he'll hit a crazy-good shot. I lost the first set in a tiebreak, won the second 6-4, and pulled out the final tiebreaker as Rich's stamina started to wane.

The court played fast. There was one service break the entire match, at 4-all in the second set. One more hold by me and the match would be even. The pressure was on. I — or, rather, my 14-year-old self — would be filled with self-loathing if I lost my serve and with it the opportunity to close out the set. And if double-faults contributed to the loss, the monster would be out of the closet and I'd have fantasies about self-strangulation.

I didn't let myself dwell on this prospect. I visualized my

stainless-steel vault where I could focus on the business of winning without a stray negative thought. I played a great game and won it. From there, it was on to the tiebreaker, which are crapshoots. At this point, though, I felt like I had the match in hand. And I did.

I walked off the court feeling good about what I'd just accomplished. I was officially if not actually the best 45+ player in the county. I'd also shown some of the match toughness I was trying to develop.

NEWBURGH, NY

My next opportunity to chase points after the College Park debacle was at a conveniently nearby location, The Powelton Club in Newburgh, NY, forty minutes down the New York State Thruway. Gary Chafetz, whom I'd beaten in Guilford, was the top seed. He'd plainly been playing a lot of tournaments because he was ranked number twelve in the country. Ed Paige, a name I was unfamiliar with, was the second (and only other) seed. His national ranking was eighteen. I was still at #24 and unseeded.

An old-style country club, The Powelton Club's rules of play required whites only. That was fine by me. The Philadelphia Grass Nationals were a few weeks away, and they had the same rule. I went out and stocked up, accessorizing with a pair of bright-red sneakers because the whites-only requirement didn't include footwear. Mavericks gotta maverick, I guess.

My first match on the red clay was against a gentleman

named Bruce Crumley. He was a nice guy and he had nice strokes – I later learned that he'd played for Texas A&M, which meant that back in the day, he could play. This was half a century later, though, and his supersenior track record, which I'd researched prior to the match, was underwhelming. Based on his technique, I expected it to be a reasonably close contest. I quickly took control, though, and prevailed one and one.

"My game is coming back," he said when we were done. "It's coming back, but slowly."

Ed Paige, the second seed, would be my next opponent. He'd played on the adjacent court while I was facing off with Crumley, against a fellow named Charles Beck who, in another Back to the Future moment, had been a practice partner for me when I was a teenager. Paige had a wicked drop shot. He also wore a brace around his left knee and limped between points. Hopefully the one would zero out the other.

I escaped, but barely. It turned out that he only limped between points. When chasing the ball, he ran just fine. His drop shot was as advertised. I missed enough to doubt my string tension and change rackets. He won the first set 6-4.

I'd have to be stubborn — I'd have to be persistent — I'd have to gut it out. The second set was close at first, but then I grabbed a lead and pulled away, winning it by 6-3. He kept flexing his right hand at the end of the set, suggesting he was cramping up, but it didn't seem to affect his play.

It was down to another pro tiebreaker. My game had solidified and momentum was on my side — I was feeling optimistic. I went ahead 9-7. Match point. I hit the ball to his forehand and he slammed it into the net just below the tape. I started to raise my arms in victory, only to watch in horror as the ball proceeded to climb two inches, seemingly of its own volition, and drop onto my side of the net. A fuzzy yellow tennis ball, risen from the dead!

9-8.

I looked in disbelief at the dozen or so people watching. The tournament director shrugged and laughed.

I had one more chance before things got really ugly. I decided to try to run him and force an error, a strategy that had started working well for me in the second set. After two or three shots back and forth, he flew a forehand long and I heaved a sigh of relief. I hadn't played great, but I'd shown match toughness at the critical moments, enough match toughness to win.

Jim Nelson was my finals opponent. He hailed from Ohio, but his son lived in New York City so he'd headed this way for a family visit coupled with some tennis. Jim is an affable guy with a big frame, an improbable head of hair for a man his age, and a deep understanding of the game. I'd spied a bit on Nelson during the semi-finals, when he'd dispatched Gary Chafetz in straight sets on the next court. He had the fluid strokes of a lifelong teaching pro, but he was also carrying some extra pounds that I thought I might be able to exploit.

That was how the match played out. I won straightfor-wardly by 6-2, 6-2. We played evenly at first, but then he started going big early in the point and missing more than he made. I got the sense that he'd decided he couldn't outsteady or outrun me, so he had to try to outgun me.

On match point, he hit to my backhand and came to net. I responded with a backhand slice down the line. He got to it and chipped it cross-court, where I chased it down. I had an opening down the line, went for it, and was gratified to see the ball go where I'd intended. Nelson got to it, but barely. His return tumbled into the bottom of the net.

I'd won the tournament and drove home elated. I'd get a big bump in the rankings.

ROSLYN HEIGHTS, NY AND SCARSDALE, NY

Mid-August delivered a new opportunity to chase points – a Cat 4 tournament at The Tennis King on Long Island. Like the College Park tournament, there'd be only one round before the finals. This time, though, the gods of the draw smiled down on me. My semi-final match would be against a player I'd defeated with the loss of only one game earlier in the year. On the other side of the draw, Alec Roberts and Michael Harvey, who'd both taken me to three sets at the May Tennis King tournament, would be facing off against each other.

I won my first match with the loss this time of three games while Alec scraped out a victory over Michael in a third-set tiebreaker. The final would be played the next weekend. We consulted with the tournament director, who graciously gave us permission to play the match at Alec's home club in Westchester, which would save us both much travel time.

We played in ideal weather on a lovely red clay court that was terraced with courts both above and below it. I beat Alec again, this time by 6-4, 6-2. I was happy with how I played, especially with my growing match toughness – I seemed to be focusing better on the important points. Alec's game blew hot and cold. There were spells when I felt helpless against him, and spells when I could count on him to miss before me.

We went out for a friendly lunch afterwards. A pair of matches had made us friends — we appeared to be kindred spirits. We both had backgrounds in journalism, we were both committed to doing good work in the world, and we were both unusually open-minded about the sort of things many people are dismissive about. He also, as he had no trouble reminding me, bore considerable responsibility for my now being ranked #11 nationally, my new status since the Red Clay Classic. If he hadn't encouraged me to keep going, I might have dropped off the supersenior circuit after my first event.

A few days later, the new rankings came out. I hadn't only made it into the top ten – I was ranked at number four.

I promptly and proudly sent a screenshot displaying my new status to friends and family who cared, and to some who probably didn't.

PHILADELPHIA, PA

All my life I've wondered: *How do I fit in? How am I alike and how am I different? What's my right place in the tribe?* While

I'm surely not alone in this – who doesn't spend at least a little time comparing themselves to the Joneses? — it may be a
more important issue for me than it is for many other people.
From elementary school through college, I was a full two years
younger than my classmates. This creates an unbreachable divide — there's no catching up with older classmates. I'd car-
ried this sense of deficit through my entire life, always feeling
like an outsider, always trying to decipher how much I fit in.

It was this lifelong question that had pushed me into
playing the supersenior circuit. I wanted to find out where I fit
in as a player – *top ten? top fifty? total stud?* – and I also wanted
to find out where I fit in as a person. What sort of people did
this unlikely community attract? How much would I enjoy my
new acquaintances? How much would they enjoy me?

My first Category 1 tournament, the Philadelphia Grass
Nationals, would be my first major opportunity to engage
these questions. The Wheeling Cat 3 tournament had attract-
ed people from afar, but this was a national championship and
it was reeling in top players from all over.

One enters the Philadelphia Cricket Club through an
arched gate. It's not pearly, but the view for a tennis player is
exhilarating, if not quite heavenly, once you're through it. On
the far side of a patio with outdoor seating, you find yourself
facing a vast meadow laid out with chalk, nets, and fencing.
Grass courts to the left, grass courts to the right, grass courts
straight ahead, twenty-some courts if you count them all. That,
plus the fact that pretty much everyone was wearing white,
transported me in my imagination to colonial Rhodesia. The

Philadelphia Cricket Club presented as an artifact of that era, all whiteness and privilege. When I happened upon a black man in a service role, I wondered how he felt about his throwback role, or if he thought about it at all.

Many tournaments give swag to the competitors. Over the course of the summer, I'd gotten tee-shirts, a coffee mug, an engraved glass mug, a polo shirt, and a thermal water bottle. The Philadelphia Cricket Club handed out tennis shirts featuring their logo, a Native American who looked strikingly similar to the controversial and no-longer-extant Washington Redskins mascot. Obliviousness seemed the order of the day. But I was here to play tennis, not stir up a fuss.

The matches were scheduled to start Tuesday. On Monday, a couple of courts were made available for practice. I hadn't played on grass for over forty years and wanted to acclimatize myself. It was less challenging than I expected. The ball tended to sit up rather than skid. The surface felt quite playable as well as easy on the legs; I'd soon find out how wrong this was.

When I headed out to the practice court, my friend Henry Kennedy, he of the big smile and even bigger personality, was there holding court – an appropriate term since he was a retired district court judge who'd recently published a memoir called *My Life on the Courts*. He introduced me to his friends, some of whom I ended up hitting with. One of them, George Deptula, I knew by reputation. He was from the Boston area and one of his regular playing partners was a guy named Laury Hammel, whom I knew from the socially responsible business community. They were an odd couple, I'd been told, with

Laury's progressive politics and George's conservative ones. Given my political biases, I approached George a bit warily, but that passed quickly. He had the biting, ironical wit of the outsider, something I recognized and appreciated.

"Oh," George said upon being introduced to me. He pointed a finger at me. "You're the guy who drove Gary Chafetz crazy."

George had a stylish game — you could get a real sense of the player he'd once been. Most 70-something tennis players use their serve to put the ball in play; they don't have the firepower to go on the attack with it. George's serve had some muscle in it, and his groundstrokes and volleys were crisp and effective. We hit it off immediately, and he got extra points when he introduced me to John Mayotte, a long-time linchpin of the community, with "he's got a nice game." These were low-key words, but an indisputable endorsement. I was a Player of Interest.

This was another Back to the Future moment for me, again with a happier ending. Just before my senior year in high school, my family moved to Washington, DC where I attended Sidwell Friends School. At my first social gathering, a football star had approached me and asked me what sports I played. I answered, with no small amount of pride, that I was a tennis player. He responded with a crestfallen look and quickly went looking for other company — it was football or nothing as far as he was concerned. Now here I was, the new kid on the block all over again, only this time all the cool kids were tennis players – and I had a 'nice game.' It was a do-over with a happy ending.

You know what they say: It's always high school in Philadelphia.

That Monday was probably the most fun day I'd had on the supersenior circuit. I didn't have a match to worry about, and I was getting to meet a bunch of guys whose company I enjoyed.

There was Tommy Walker, a teaching pro from Westchester County not far from where I live, a rail-thin, gentlemanly, ridiculously fit 76-year-old who was a living testament to the power of eating only fruit, which he claimed to do.

There was Wes Jackson, in from California, a short, slender fellow I got in some practice games against, winning a point, or maybe two, in the process.

There was Rod Schroeder, a teaching pro from the Chicago area who ended up advancing reasonably far in the tournament.

The seeded players had years of experience, long lists of wins against strong players, and in some cases high honors like representing their country. Bob Litwin was the top seed. Tim Griffin from Toronto had represented Canada in multiple international competitions. I was unseeded despite my national ranking. This seemed fair, given my thin track record.

My first-round draw pitted me against, of all people, Gary Chafetz. If I won, I'd play Denny Posteraro or Gary Jenkins in the next round. It would either be a revenge match or a test against the best. It would be fun either way, but I'd have to get through Chafetz first.

Our match unspooled much like the one at Guilford. It was a muggy day and the match felt like a slog. It took a while to finish, but the score ended comfortably in my favor.

The next day would bring the test I'd been looking forward to all season. I'd be playing Gary Jenkins, who'd dispatched Denny Posteraro by the same score I'd beaten Chafetz.

It was clear what I'd have to do. I'd advanced as far as I had in the rankings by being able to outrun and outsteady my opponents. This wouldn't work against Jenkins, who someone had described as a "machine." He didn't get tired and he didn't miss. If I were to have a shot at winning, I'd have to play muscular, aggressive tennis – grass court tennis, in other words. I couldn't just throw my serve in. I'd have to bang it, and be aggressive on both the first and second. I'd need to serve and volley enough to let him know I might attack at any time. Grass wasn't his forte. If I could summon enough courage and match toughness to play off my front foot, and if, early on, I could hit some shots that gave me confidence, I might have a shot at beating him.

It rained overnight and the schedule got shuffled. I got to the club before noon, believing that my match was scheduled for 1:30. At 12:30, the tournament director started calling out names. I paid him no mind — I wouldn't be playing till an hour later.

I was relaxing in a nearby chair when Jim Nelson happened by. He looked startled to see me. "You should be playing! Gary's out on the court waiting for you."

Either I'd misread the schedule or it had been changed

after I looked at it. I grabbed my bag and hustled out onto the court, beating a formal default by a bare few minutes.

Standing across the net from a person is a very different experience from watching from the sidelines. The first few games were a feeling-out process for me, and perhaps for him as well. He hit a topspin second serve, which struck me as a bit risky, but he didn't miss it and he placed his shots well. I didn't feel overmatched, and while I wasn't anywhere close to being in the zone, I felt pretty solid out there and figured I'd work my way into the match. We both held serve and then he held to go up 2-1. We played a couple of tight games, both of which he won. On one game point, I hit a hard second serve that felt great off the racket but landed a fraction of an inch deep. On another, he hit a lob that I didn't see land and didn't dare call out although it may have been. Matches are won and lost on such minutiae. It still felt like a pretty even match, but he was up now by 4-1.

About three games in, my hip had started screaming at me. I was learning the hard way how difficult it is to play on grass. A lot of shots stay low, which means you have to bend deep at the knees and twist from the hips to strike the ball. My ultra-tight right hip decided that was a really bad idea and let me know it on most shots, especially my serve, which I have to really rotate into for it to be effective.

I asked an observing USTA official if I could get an on-court trainer. None was available. If I'd had my wits about me, I'd have popped four ibuprofen, but I had tennis, not medicine, on my mind – and it probably wouldn't have mattered anyway because my hip continued to natter at me for a full month after the tournament.

Playing in pain is doubly challenging because in addition to forcing you to adjust physically, it takes one's mind away from strategy and execution and turns it to pain management. The game passed in a blur. Moments later, it was 5-1.

It had been clear to me for a couple of games that I'd probably have to retire. I might have been able to stagger through against a clearly inferior adversary. Not with Jenkins, though, who, so far as I knew, hadn't lost a set all year.

I walked to the net, motioned him to join me there, and stuck out my hand.

"It's my hip," I said. "I'm done."

"Really? I hadn't noticed." Then he said, "With that twist second serve of yours, do you ever double fault?"

"Gary," I said, "you have no idea."

We walked off the court together. His undefeated streak was still intact — I was still trying to sort out my feelings. The match had ended abruptly, in an unexpected way, with the score heavily in his favor. What was I to make of it? I didn't think the score accurately reflected the tightness of the contest, and I believe Gary agreed because I'm pretty sure I overheard him say to John Mayotte a few minutes later, "I played a guy named Carl Frankel. He could beat me."

That could have meant many things, of course, if it hadn't just been my overwrought imagination at work and he'd actually said it. It might have meant that I was in the "I could beat him when I'm at my best and he's at his worst" category.

I didn't hear it that way, though. I believe he was saying that I was at his level.

Now I knew what to make of the match.

It was confirmed: I was a Player of Interest.

I'd come to Philadelphia bearing my age-old question, which over time had evolved into my old-age question: *Where do I fit in?* On paper, I hadn't done well, but I left feeling good about the answer.

Twenty Questions on the Road to Mastery

It takes a long time to develop mastery. The usual rule of thumb is 10,000 hours of practice. That adds up to four hours a day, every day, for about seven years.

My personal experience confirms how slow progress can be. Since returning to the court six years ago, I've probably had about 1,500 on-court sessions. I've definitely gotten better. But how much? I'd estimate that I've improved by 10-15%. One thousand five hundred sessions, fifteen percent improvement: That adds up to getting better by one-tenth of one percent each time I played.

One-tenth of one percent.

How many balls have I hit per session? Surely more than 1,000. That adds up to a million and a half separate practice opportunities. That's a whole lot of ball-striking for very little progress. Pursuing mastery is such a slog that I've wondered at times if it's worth the effort, especially when one is of a certain age and fighting entropy along with technical and physical shortcomings.

My occasional dark night of the tennis soul tends to last for minutes, not hours. Put those little shards of melancholy aside and I am convinced that the pursuit of mastery is unequivocally worth it.

First, as a zillion wise people have said before me, there

is no destination. The reward lies in the journey. A famous —
and, for the 1950s, sexually suggestive — line from a Cunard
steamship company read: "Getting there is half the fun!" Well,
sure — and it's *all* the fun when there's no final destination.
That's what a practice is, after all — an ongoing commitment
to the doing, not the getting done.

Second, the snail-like rate of progress helps us climb up
the ladder of time and become more comfortable with a lon-

ger perspective. It takes us out of the Immediate Now and teaches *patience*, which is a must-have on the road to wisdom. There can be no forcing the spring.

The lack of positive feedback we get about our progress can actually be seen as a positive. "No appointments, no disappointments," the famous spiritual teacher Muktananda is reputed to have said. When session after session passes and we don't feel like we're getting better, it returns us to the basic verities. *Do it for the doing of it. Keep plugging away and trust the process.* Persisting becomes an act of faith, and at the end of the day, it is faith — in God, in one's friends, in one's personal choices, and for me, faith in the practice of tennis — that fuels and inspires us.

Last but by no means least, the question must be asked: *Mastery at what?* I adopted tennis as a formal if somewhat idiosyncratic spiritual practice — as a moving meditation, if you will — because I wanted to get better at tennis. That was my main impetus, but I also saw it as an opportunity to confront my frailties and fallibilities while also embracing my more brag-friendly qualities in a context that was fun and therapeutic. I practice tennis to become more masterful at life as well as at tennis.

Ask yourself the twenty questions of this chapter honestly and kindly, be ready to practice self-forgiveness every step along the way, and over time you may find that the inquiry has helped clear out some of the psychological noise that slows your progress both on the court and in your life.

One final note: I chose twenty as a number for one reason

only — because 'twenty questions' is a familiar meme. I was fitting this chapter inside a tradition, so to speak. I could have had ten questions, and I could have had forty.

There is no order of importance, either.

You are cordially invited to come up with your own questions.

#1: WHAT ARE YOUR CORE ISSUES AND HOW DO THEY SHOW UP ON THE TENNIS COURT?

A map of your neuroses: What a fun thing to do! Only the characterization isn't fair or accurate. A psychological issue can arise from how you're wired as well as from how you're miswired. So: What about you gets in your way when you're playing tennis?

I will swallow hard and lead by example.

I grew up in an academic-intellectual Jewish family. It was assumed by all that I was the Second Coming of my indisputably brilliant father. In ways, however, I felt impossibly stupid. I couldn't find things to save my life. I couldn't figure out how to fit two pieces of plumbing pipe together. To my teachers and my parents and their friends, I was a boy genius. To me, not so much.

When I was ten, I wrote a play about a boy named Reinhold. It was called 'Boy Genius.' What a coincidence! During almost the entire five minutes of performance time, Reinhold's mother is bragging to her best friend about how smart her son is. She is so proud of him and how couldn't she be? Because he is, like, a *total* genius.

The climax comes when Reinhold stumbles onto the stage. He isn't a genius — he's a dork. His glasses are askew and his laces are untied. He says, "Mom, where's my shoe?"

She looks at him adoringly and says, "It's on your foot, dear."

Now cue the cultural cluelessness: Not only did my teacher give me an A when I handed in this mini-play, but the powers that be decided that it should be performed for the entire school community and that I should play Reinhold as a testament to my brilliance.

Not a single soul noticed what in retrospect was a loud and obvious cry to be heard — a cry to be seen — your proverbial cry for help.

And there, friends, you have in a nutshell the story of Carl's Imposter Syndrome, which was compounded by the fact that from the fifth grade on, I was two years younger than my classmates and had to pretend that I was as old and mature as they were.

When I was fifteen, I played a kid in a 16-and-under tournament in northern New Jersey. He was one of those kids who couldn't possibly beat me on his best day and my worst day — only this time, he did. Personally, I blame my father, who'd come along that day to provide chauffeur services and, in theory, emotional support. In fact, though, all his presence really accomplished, although all he did was stand impassively at courtside, was to drive the volume up to 11 on my Imposter-Meter. I won the first set handily, somehow managed to lose the second, and said to my dad before the final set started: "If I lose to this guy, I swear I'll flush my head down the toilet."

You probably know how the match ended up. The ride home from New Jersey was a silent nightmare, steeped in horror and in shame. The myth of the glorious son, the prince, the star, the stud, had been exposed. The gauze of my glory had been torn off my wound and a fetid pit — my true self! — had been revealed.

And then I double-shamed myself by not keeping my pledge to my father by keeping my head, literally if not figuratively, on my shoulders.

Fast-forward to almost sixty years later. It's been a long journey to get from "you must pretend or you will die" to "you will die if you pretend." Somehow I've managed to get there — I see it as the most important accomplishment of my life. Those old stories still hang around, though.

My match against Phil Roholt in the consolation finals at the Jack Dorsey Memorial in Wheeling recapitulated this event. I mean no disrespect to Phil, who played smart and solid tennis from the second set on. I wanted to win the match and, almost as importantly, to make a good impression on the onlookers whose community I was joining, just as I'd hoped to impress my father over five decades ago. As you may recall, I did manage to scrape out a win, but I'd left the court with my shoulders hunched up around my neck, feeling unhappy and ashamed about how my game had regressed.

My imposter story had been activated. It was only mildly painful compared to the agony of 56 years earlier. Now, thank goodness, I had tools to manage my upset: Ironic distancing (my embarrassing performance had been what my wife and I call "another fucking growth opportunity"), a sense of context (in the grand scheme, this was insignificance piled on insignificance), self-compassion ("so you have issues, Carl — join the crowd"), gratitude (another opportunity to confront my demon). And humor! Fate had decided to mess with me and come up with a real thigh-slapper.

Still, the scab had been torn off the wound. We all have vampires, and they don't die easily.

Okay: You've made out a list, both naughty and nice. You've identified your core issues. Now what? How do you take this information and turn it into progress on and off the tennis court?

First, you congratulate yourself on your achievement. Making a list is not nothing — it sets you on the road toward greater self-awareness and self-mastery.

Second, you practice noticing these issues when they arise. This must be followed by direct action, which in this context means three things:

- *Consciously countering a negative thought with a positive one.* Let's say I've just had a run of forehand errors and the thought arises: "This isn't going to be my day." I note the thought and quote the iconic Rolling Stones lyric to myself, more than once if I have to: "It's just a shot away." Meaning: "Give me one good forehand and confidence will flow in, transforming my day."

- *Consciously closing the door to negative thoughts.* Let's say I'm deep into a close set, the score is 30-40, and I have to hit a second serve. I think, "If I double-fault, it'll prove that I'm a choker." I notice the thought and speak sternly, as if to a child: "Negative thought, you're not welcome here. Not now." I then imagine that thought, like a child outside its parents' locked bedroom, turning around and walking away. Sometimes "no means no" for real.

- *Being consciously physical.* One way to compensate for negative thoughts is to get more embodied. Bounce! Skip! Activate those bones ...

None of these countermeasures are time-consuming. A single corrective thought requires nanoseconds, bouncing up and down a mere second or two. None of this will happen, though, without a prior noticing. Progress starts with self-awareness.

It's not easy to be in witness mode while engaged in what an ancient part of ourselves experiences as a life-and-death struggle for survival. It requires the ability to toggle between two different points on the continuum of time — the Immediate Now and up-mountain a piece. But that, precisely, is one of the things that makes tennis such a great practice. I'm reminded of the perhaps-apocryphal story about the High Abbot of a Buddhist monastery who many centuries ago was confronted by a great general who'd invaded his country and stormed into his abbey at the head of his vast army.

"Do you know who I am?" says the military man. "I am" — he gives his name — "and I can cut your head off without blinking an eye."

"Do you know who I am?" says the High Abbot. "I am" — he gives his name — "and I can watch you cut my head off without blinking an eye."

Wouldn't it be nice to play tennis that way?

What are your core issues? How do they show up on the tennis court?

#2: WHAT NEGATIVE STORIES ARISE WHEN YOU COMPETE?

Snakes shed skins. Humans shed stories, narratives that we adopted when we were young to explain the world we found ourselves in. But that comes with a caveat. *Conscious* humans shed stories. People who stay unconscious about the narratives they impose on the world tend to stay stuck inside them:

- "Dad is great except for when he's drunk, when he insults me and hits me" turns into "all men are unpredictable, violent and not to be trusted." This is the sort of story, tragic in origin, that creates self-defeating patterns if allowed to guide one's life.

- "Mom didn't hold me when I was upset" becomes "Mom never holds me when I'm upset," which becomes "Nobody really cares about how I feel," which becomes the nonsensical charge, delivered like a clash of cymbals at the height of an argument with one's spouse, "You don't care about me and you never did!"

The extent to which people spend their lives in thrall to their old stories — or, alternatively, climb above them — goes a long way toward determining whether they get wiser or more shrunken as they age. Some people successfully shed their skins. They outgrow themselves, so to speak, and take their place in society as its elders. Other people stay stuck in Childish-Mind — they become more ingrown. These are the cranky old men yelling, "Get off my lawn!"

One of the Childish-Mind narratives I bring onto the court is: *He's just too good. I'll never beat him.* Sometimes, of course, this is actually true. If I were to go out against Roger Federer … even a limping, retired Roger Federer … even a limping, retired Roger Federer who was shackled at the ankles, the dude would thump me. There are times, though, when the thought is nonsensical, the unfortunate consequence of a schooling situation where I was looking uphill at my older classmates and I couldn't do a damn thing about it.

All this renders me vulnerable to descending into hopelessness. Now, when I notice this old narrative arising, I counter it as best I can.

You've got more game than you think.

It's a game of momentum swings.

Sometimes I add my childhood nickname to my inner reminders. It gives my self-talk more oomph.

You've got more game than you think, Rookie.

It's a game of momentum swings. Rook.

I'm not conning myself with these pep talks. They're actually true. It's my Childish-Mind that's the bullshit artist.

What old stories do you bring to the court? And what can you do about them?

#3. IN WHAT WAYS DOES YOUR PERSONALITY DEFINE YOUR GAME?

Who we are determines how we play, for better and for worse.

Some personality models provide luminous clarity about ourselves and others. One such model is the Enneagream, which was developed by the early 20th Century spiritual teacher George Gurdjieff. The Enneagram identifies nine personality types, which are identified by number and linked in ways that are too various and complex to address here. Each of the nine types has strengths and weaknesses, each type can be more or less evolved, and all are created equal. Enneagram experts name the nine types differently — the following list is representative:

1. The Idealist

2. The Helper

3. The Achiever

4. The Artist

5. The Observer

6. The Loyalist

7. The Enthusiast

8. The Dominator

9. The Mediator

Again, I'll put myself front and center. I am an Ennea-gram Five, an "Observer," also called the "Witness." I tend to approach things from the point of view of the outsider whose first impulse is to watch, not do. I'm wired for voyeurism in everything I do. I suspect it's due to both nature and nurture. I was born that way, and I spent my childhood and college years on the outside looking in — or, more precisely, two years younger looking up.

Of late, I've come to enjoy being an Enneagram Five. I've gotten over the notion that I'm insufficiently in touch with my feelings and started liking myself for who I am. My predispo-sition to be in witness mode means that my default position tends to be high-level and inclusive — it encourages analytical clarity and a healthy sense of context — I'm less prone to the madness of crowds than your more in-the-moment person. But there are also downsides to being a Five. The boundary between thinking and doing gets blurred even more easily than with your average non-Five bear. Embodying is a special challenge for us, especially when it's matched by an intelligence type that isn't primarily kinesthetic, as is the case for me.

The mind-body split: It's a bitch, especially for Observers.

I do my best to cope with this challenge by giving myself verbal instructions that are designed to engage and activate my body. Before a point starts, I may decide to play the short-stop who's going to spring into gear and take off after the ball the moment he picks up its trajectory. If I'm playing doubles and my partner is serving, I'll resolve to move two steps forward the moment I see his ball pass by me. Sometimes I'll skip up and down a couple of times before preparing to serve, just like the big boys and girls do.

I'll never stop being a Witness, but I can get better at milking it for its benefits and not letting its challenges get in the way.

Other personality types will encounter different challenges. An Enneagram Eight (the Boss, the Dominator) might have to dial back their tendency to try to muscle through every challenge. An Enneagram Two (the Helper) might need to actively practice getting comfortable with dictating.

You don't need to be into psychological models, the Enneagram or anything else, to do this. All you need is the introspective capacity to match personality traits with performance characteristics.

Who you are tells you what you need to work on.

In what ways does your personality structure correlate with your performance on the tennis court? How can you better leverage the inherent strengths of who you are while reducing the impact of its problematic qualities?

#4. WHAT ARE YOUR MOST VEXING MENTAL ERRORS?

Again, I'll use myself as an example. My top two are: 1) I don't chase the ball until I've decided it's going in, and 2) I assume the point is won and stand there contemplating my victory rather than preparing to return a ball that still may come back to me.

These aren't only errors — they are sins, if we take the improbable step of migrating these bad habits into a moral universe. They are both the sin of sloth.

How do I find virtue on the tennis court? As it happens, the Christian tradition brings us seven virtues along with the seven sins. One of them is diligence. That's the ticket for me — *play each point until it's done.*

How do I get there? Again, with affirmations before each point that undercut my penchant for laziness.

Instead of "I'd rather not run if I can help it" — *"I play each point as if it were the last point in my life."*

Instead of "I'll assume I've won the point if I've hit what looks like a winner" — *"I play every point until it's over."*

Instead of "I'll try to remember to work hard" — *"I'm a professional, and professionals do their job relentlessly."*

We'll never stop making mental errors. We can sharply reduce their frequency, though.

What mental errors do you commit repeatedly on the court? What counter-narratives will help you get past them?

#5: WHAT IS YOUR ON-COURT RELATIONSHIP WITH ANGER?

Anger is a challenging and complex emotion. It has its virtues — I'm glad people get mad when they encounter injustice. But it's as gooey as quicksand. Anger can harden into grievances that shape our character in sad ways. Anger doesn't do well with being repressed — it tends to show up anyway, often more loudly and inappropriately than if attempts weren't being made to squash it. If expressed unskillfully, which is usually the case, it only makes for more unhappiness. Anger can corrode our soul and destroy our relationships. And yet it has a draw, a sweet reward. There's nothing like righteous anger to give us a sense of power and purpose.

For some people, anger has an addictive quality — the term 'anger-holic' exists for a reason. It's an emotional survival strategy for them — better to be uplifted by the winds of rage than to tumble into despondency and despair. Others run screaming from their anger, which they experience as undermining their commitment to live in peace, turn the other cheek, etc. The vast majority of people, I think, work hard to control their anger but sometimes get triggered and explode.

The tennis court gives us a great opportunity to fine-tune our relationship with anger. It certainly gives us reason to feel it! We can get angry with ourselves — I *missed that shot again!* We can get angry at our opponent — *I'm sure my shot was in!* We can get angry with the gods — *that's three net-cord winners for my opponent and not a single one for me!* Thus the question arises: What do we do with this feeling when it arises?

There isn't a single right answer. John McEnroe used it effectively for fuel. Others do their best to not get riled up, both on general principle and because they believe they play better that way.

There are really two conversations here. First, how does anger affect your performance? Second, how does it affect your opponent? It's one thing to *feel* anger, and it's another to express it to whoever you are expressing it to — your opponent, your audience, the world at large, the shadow of your mom and dad. If you lose your serve, it's within the range of appropriateness to hit your spare ball across the net with a bit of extra force. But this requires a modicum of self-control, and the thing about anger is that it has a will toward no self-control; it tips easily into conduct that is inconsiderate, inappropriate, and just plain ill-advised.

Negative energy is infectious, and tennis is a shared activity. When I play *against* an opponent, I am also playing with them. We are in a sort of dance together, and when I'm swearing loudly at myself or otherwise letting the world know how unhappy I am with myself (or my opponent, or the gods), it can make the game less fun for them.

For me, this makes a compelling case against acting out. Civility matters.

There's another reason not to do it. Out-of-control expressions of anger are communications of frustration — they reveal a fear of losing. What can be more bracing than knowing that the person across from you is feeling on the ropes?

Less fun, more confidence — this isn't a combo you want to be handing your opponent. It's not considerate of either of you.

Does anger arise on the tennis court for you? When it does, how do you manage it? Might there be a healthier way to be in relationship with it, and if so, what would it look like?

#6: WHAT IS YOUR ON-COURT RELATIONSHIP WITH SHAME?

A regular practice partner confessed something to me the other day. He's reluctant to come to the net because he's terrified of being beaten by a lob. "There's nothing more humiliating than that," he said.

He has a perfectly serviceable volley and overhead. He is capable of performing at least as well as me at net because he daily commits the crime of being younger than I am and is therefore quicker to cover passing shots and, yes, lobs.

Just as some cars are 'pre-owned,' my friend 'pre-defeats' himself with his fear of being shamed.

As we've seen, shame has a big presence in my inner life, too. This, for me, has transformed tennis into a sort of scrubbing practice wherein I work at reconciling myself to my failures and at becoming genuinely okay with points or matches that push my shame button.

Although personal-growth teachers often stress the importance of 'ridding ourselves of shame,' I don't share that view. We *should* feel shame if we do something deplorable. People who can't feel shame are sociopaths. But there is healthy shame and there is pathological shame. The only healthy shame on the tennis court is produced by bad behavior — throwing your racket, cheating, etc. Shame at how you're playing (or, in my friend's case, at how you're losing points) is always pathological.

Which doesn't make it easier to scrub.

Is there shame in your game? What can you do about it?

#7: HOW DO YOU DEAL WITH YOUR ON-COURT FAILURES?

Failure, like you-know-what, happens. There's probably not a soul on earth who doesn't experience a "drat" when they miss. But then many of us then turn that transient emotion into a narrative of failure.

I can't do anything right today.

I just can't put the ball away.

These are emotions disguised as reality statements, emotions dragged up out the muck of the Immediate Now to a broader and more absolute narrative: I *suck*.

Since Roger Federer misses shots, this must mean that he sucks, too.

This is one of the main mistakes that Childish-Mind makes. It races at the speed of light from the individual instance to the absolute truth.

Mommy ignored me — Mommy always ignored me.

This is the logical fallacy known as the 'hasty generalization.' Childish-Mind stories are not to be trusted.

I missed an easy shot — I always miss the easy shots.

Errors can be instructive. There is something to be learned from every shot you miss. Why did you misfire? Was it physical? Was it mental? What can you do to correct it? Although it's generally thought that you should jettison your error-correction program when you compete and just play, I don't believe that notion has merit below the true elite. For one thing, we common folk aren't good enough to go on full automatic pilot, and for another, the instruction set I send my body when I prepare to hit a shot usually relates back to a prior one: If it's a slice approach down the line, I tell myself something like, "Hit it like last time, only turn your shoulder more."

On rare occasions, I'm actively grateful when I screw up because it sheds such a bright and embarrassing light on what I'm doing wrong that it operates like a Zen knock upside the head and ensures that I won't make the same error again any time soon. Like that time during a friendly social match when I had an overhead a foot away from the net and missed the ball completely: General hilarity ensued, topped by a rush of embarrassment on my part, completed by the staggering realization that I'd taken my eye off the ball completely. The debacle helped me more than a garden-variety screw-up would have. It brought me back to watching the ball again.

Do you befriend your errors? Do you make narratives out of them? Do you recognize your Childish-Mind when it speaks?

#8: HOW DO YOU DEAL WITH YOUR ON-COURT SUCCESSES?

Two sides of the same coin: Fear of success, fear of failure. Fall down, and someone will stomp you upside the head. Rise up, and you're headed for a fall. Both are drawn from the same well: Fear of the future.

A lot of us sabotage ourselves when we're playing well or on the verge of success. We assume it's a done deal and start coasting too early, or we scare ourselves half to death at the thought of how awful we'll feel if we tighten up and lose *now*.

It's not only us hackers and semi-hackers who face this challenge. A half-century ago, Marty Riessen was one of the world's best players. I remember an interview with him when he said after coming back from an injury, "After a layoff like I had, I had to learn to win again."

It's not uncommon to have mixed feelings about winning.

It's a status that's charged with meanings that we project onto it:

- Success as an unequivocal positive. *I've made it to the top. Rest awaits me; I can finally lay my burden down.*

- A mixed bag — success equals respect, a good thing, and it also equals grasping for success — not so hot. *I will be looked up to and admired by others.*

- Success as a recipe for failure. *I've flown too close to the sun and will crash and burn eventually.* Also: *I've set a standard I'll have trouble matching again.*

Success can be as challenging as failure. Recently, I had a spell when my second serve was on fire. I couldn't seem to double-fault no matter what I did — and I was going for it. Day after day passed, and set after set after set.

Typically, when I line up to hit my second serve, I endure a brief encounter with the forces of darkness. *Will this be the time I screw up?* During my hot spell, I asked the same question for a while, and then I stopped asking it because the likelihood of it happening seemed so low. Eventually my success started making me crazy. The suspense was getting to be too much for me: *This has to end soon. When will I crash and burn?*

The altitude was too much for me. Success had mutated into stress.

(Succ-stress?)

There soon followed, predictably, my swan dive into failure. I started hitting my second serve while focusing on the prospect of failure rather than on the stroke itself. When you visualize failure, that's what you're more likely to get.

When I finally double-faulted, I felt actively relieved. It got the monkey off my back.

Does success come easily for you? If not, why not? And what can you do about it?

#9: HOW DO YOU FEEL ABOUT COMPETING?

Competing against another person is not the same as competing against yourself. It's pecking-order stuff, and it's public, not private. Shame and plaudits await you, or seem to.

It's only natural to get nervous before a match. Bill Russell, the legendary basketball center, threw up before *every* match he played. At the 2017 Wimbledon championships, which he would win without losing a single set, Federer lost his serve early in the first set of his first match against Dusan Lajovic of Serbia. When asked to explain what happened, he answered, "This is Wimbledon. I was nervous."

This after winning seven Wimbledon championships.

I experience match nervousness as a pervasive physical tightness, as if my body is resisting what I'll be asking it to do. Many years ago, a therapist told me about a patient of his who knew that a session would end with a commitment to leave his wife. His leg broke spontaneously on the way up the stairs.

That's how my body feels on the way to a tough match. It's the sort of feeling that, if I were five years old, would have been followed by my jumping up and down and hollering, "I don't wanna, mommy!"

But of course I do wanna, more than not, or else I wouldn't be competing.

I can only surmise what super-jocks like Federer and Russell were afraid of, but I assume they were beyond the fear of shame and that their anxiety was about underperforming (missing one's target on a crucial shot, failing to snag that all-important rebound) and losing as a result. My nervousness has more neurotic underpinnings. I'm afraid I'll leave the court hating myself.

I don't always completely get over my nervousness. When it lingers, it takes the form of held breath, constrained stroke production, and excessively cautious strategizing. Still, I've been told I compete well more than not. The physical pleasures of tennis usually take over, the worry recedes, and I start doing my thing, more or less successfully. The reality of competition supersedes the fantasy of failure.

Do you get nervous before you compete? The right amount of nervous? What steps can you take to control — or make the most of — your nerves?

#10: WHO DO YOU PLAY FOR?

There is a 'duh' aspect to this question: For ourselves, of course. But there are others.

If I'm playing before an audience, I'm playing for them, too. I want them to think I'm a good player. I want them to think I'm a gentleman on the court — courtly on the court, if you will. I want to perform admirably for them by every reasonable measure. (If 'admirable' means hitting your forehand like the now-retired Juan Martin del Potro, they'll have to look elsewhere.)

I play for my opponent(s). I want them to enjoy their time on the court with me. I want them to think I've got game.

I play for my friends and supporters. I want to validate their faith in me.

I play for the once-real and now-imaginary beings who still inhabit my soul. My deceased parents, for example. They've been dead for over 40 years and I still want to make them proud.

Not all our audiences help us play better. I've had moments when I wonder if I compete worse because of my desire to show my opponent a good time. My nice-guy impulses may make it harder for me to dominate with delight.

What audiences do you play for? How do they affect your game? If they cause you to play worse, what can you do about it?

#11: HOW HEALTHY IS YOUR RELATIONSHIP WITH THE CONTINUUM OF TIME?

Tennis drags us into the Immediate Now. If I'm playing a match against someone who's clearly weaker than I am and I go down 2-1 in the first set, I start to stress out. *Is this a portent of the nightmare to come? Will I get tight and choke?* It doesn't take much for my imagination to start spinning shameful scenarios.

I'm not panicking when this happens — I'm making sure I don't panic. I'm using anxiety to metabolize the biochemical reactions that arise as I come to terms with the fact that I will have to switch out of cruise control into fight-or-flight mode — like it or not, I'm in a tennis war. I'm summoning the necessary adrenaline.

Adrenaline, you're a monster.

Adrenaline, you're a savior.

Adrenaline, you're a bitch.

In the match I'm imagining, I'm clearly the better player. Anyone watching who knows tennis also knows that my falling behind is a blip in the course of the inevitable outcome, which is that I'll win — I just have way too much game. But that is a higher-level perspective, and as such it's not available to me at that moment because I've been sucked into the intensity of the Immediate Now.

The very best competitors possess a remarkable ability that I can only aspire to. They can focus fully on the urgency of each shot and point while also, at a meta-level, maintaining a healthy sense of context.

Roger Federer's capacity to 'duplex' is an essential part of his tennis genius. After losing two championship points in the 15-13 fifth set of the 2018 Wimbledon final against Novak Djokovic, and ultimately the match itself, he said, "I got over it in a few days. After all, it's only tennis."

Do you get too caught up in the Immediate Now? How good are you at duplexing?

#12: ARE YOU A DANCER OR A DOMINATOR?

It's been said that reality is what you make of it. That's certainly true on the tennis court where our relationship with the person or people across the net has a double aspect. As noted above, they're both our partner and our opponent.

Our partner, you say? Isn't our partner the person who's on *our* side of the net? That depends on what we mean by 'partner.' Some people are more fun to play and practice against than others. Your styles are compatible — you dance well together, so to speak. It is in this sense that the person across the net is your partner.

When you play and also when you compete, to what extent do you do it for the joy and beauty of the dance, and to what extent do you do it because you want to walk off the court feeling like you were the better player? Do you play to dance or do you play to dominate?

Clearly, this is not an either/or proposition. If you love tennis, it's probably partly because you love the dance. At a subtle level, however, the dancer-vs.-dominator mix you bring to the court can provide insight into both how (and why) you play and into how you can play better. Let's say you're in a rally. You've gotten your opponent out of position. Now all you need to do is hit the ball into the open court and the point is yours. How consistent are you at doing this? Do you make an inordinate amount of errors when you try?

Hitting into an opening is a very different exercise from hitting the ball back to a person. I tilt so much toward dancing that it's harder for me to hit into space than it is to return it to my partner. In fact, this is so true for me that I sometimes envision imaginary opponents on the order of imaginary friends who are standing in the open space where I need to hit the ball to win the point. I find it easier to chip it to a person, if only in my imagination, than to hit into a clear opening.

When you have a chance to go directly at an opponent, for instance when they're at the net and you get a weak second serve, do you thrive on trying to hit it through the person at the net? Do you sometimes go for it even when it may not be the best choice of shot? Do you do it because you enjoy the rush that comes with overpowering your opponent? If so, you're probably more of a dominator.

If you're a dominator, might there be times to back off this approach? If you're a dancer, are there steps you might take to increase your competitive effectiveness?

#13: ARE YOU MORE INTO CONTROL OR INTO FREEDOM?

"If you love someone, set them free. If they come back to you, it was meant to be."
- Richard Bach, Jonathan Livingston Seagull

Roughly a half-century ago, the media philosopher Marshall McLuhan defined technology as any apparatus, contraption or invention that extends the power and reach of our bodies and our senses. A tennis racket fits this definition neatly. It makes our arm longer and enables us to smack the ball much harder and further than we could if we were using our hand.

Racket technology has come a long way. The modern tennis racket supports enormous amounts of power as well as enormous amounts of control, assuming you have the right technique and training. Modern-day sticks are a beast.

Speaking very generally, we can relate to our technologies in either of two ways. We can attempt to expand on them, release their power if you will — and we can try to control them to make sure we don't use their agency to do something stupid. Nukes provide a great example of this. For going on a century, we've been making them more powerful while also trying to control them in ways that make them more secure by limiting access, protesting their existence, etc.

Now let's return to the nano-nuke you're holding in your hand. You basically have the same two options: Make sure it doesn't misbehave — hold on tight, as it were — or enable and encourage it to do its thing.

Release the kraken, so to speak.

I grew up trying mostly to control the beast. Here I was with a new and considerably longer arm — my challenge was to find the ball with my new 'hand,' strike it in the center of the racket (my new 'palm'), and take it from there.

This approach — *Control! Control!* — has been my tennis Prime Directive for over fifty years.

Recently I had a sort of mini-revelation — there is another way. I could shift my paradigm from control to liberation. I could empower my technology (Yonex, as it happens) by focusing on doing the sort of things that let it be, as they say, all it can be. Things like a wrist lag-and-snap, a lighter grip, and using my big muscles.

I could embrace, in other words, the basics of the modern game. And that is what, with mixed success, I've been trying to do — shift from a paradigm of control to a paradigm of power.

Where does your psyche tilt, toward liberation or control? Where do you want it to be? What's your sweet spot? Your bleeding edge?`

#14: DO YOU HAVE ENOUGH *LI* IN YOUR GAME?

Imagine a river flowing between its banks. The river is *chi* — movement, energy — and the banks are *li* — the structure that contains and directs the water. They're inseparable like *yin* and *yang*. You can't have one without the other.

Structure is what allows energy to achieve its fullest potential. Think of the tango, which is the sexy dance it is precisely because it's so rich with *li*. The erotic energy emerges distilled and steaming through the tight formal structures of the dance.

Tennis at its best is a dance of *li* and *chi*. Consider the modern forehand. The unit turn provides structure, as does the left arm squared off in front of the body, fingers aimed at the incoming ball. The expression of *chi* that is the actual swing is rendered as explosive as it is by the layers of surrounding structure, which it blasts through.

In late November of 2021, I had a hitting session at a Florida tournament under the eye of the savant-like coach of the guys I was practicing with. One of his recommendations was that I engage my left arm more on my forehand. What he was saying, essentially, was that I should stop treating my off-arm like an unfortunate and unwelcome appendage, sort of like the little sister who's decided to tag along on a hot date. The point he drove home was that the off-arm isn't merely something that you want to keep from getting in the way. You want to put it to work by having it add structure to your forehand. When you fail to engage the off-arm enough, your *chi* lacks enough *li* and you are left flailing.

Beginning and intermediate players tend to disregard *li* and focus on the non-trivial challenge of getting to the ball and then hitting the damn thing back. The more adept you get at tennis, the more it becomes a choreographed dance defined by formal structures — footwork patterns, early preparation, wrist lag-and-snap — that are developed and refined over time.

Structure is a hallmark of excellence. It is also something we can consciously choose to focus on, or not.

Do you bring the right amount of structure to your tennis game? How about in life?

#15: WHERE DO YOU DRAW YOUR ENERGY AND INSPIRATION FROM?

Again, I'll offer myself as an example. I draw energy and inspiration from three distinct sources. First, from myself, or rather from my own ego ideal. Who do I want to be when I play? I imagine a person who is gracious, self-contained, bold, and impervious to pressure. Gary Cooper, if you will, or Brad Pitt. I then try to method-act my way into that identity. Playing 'as if' brings me closer to my ideal than I'd get if I weren't. It's how I hoist myself up by my bootstraps.

How about you? Are you drawn to sports role-play?

I also have my tennis heroes. When my will starts to flag, I invoke the never-say-die attitude of Rafael Nadal, who plays every point like it's the last point of his life.

These are archetypes. Gary Cooper and Brad Pitt are Gentleman Warriors. Rafa Nadal is a demi-god of perseverance.

My third option is also an archetype, but of a different kind. When my game is off, when it — and I — feel lost in the thickets, I invoke the idea of Beauty.

"Be beautiful," I tell myself, which while perhaps not the most memorable catch-phrase of all time, is certainly better than "Be best."

What happens when I tell myself this? First, I lighten up. There's humor in it because 'beauty' is usually associated with females, and — trust me on this — I would not make a pretty woman. Next, I slow down. Striving to be beautiful, or at a minimum graceful, takes me off automatic pilot. My mind and body separate in a good way. I perceive my execution more holistically, for one thing, and for another my execution is hitched to a more inspiring goal than 'hit it into the forehand corner.' It's an esthetic goal, and it's premised on the notion that esthetic excellence translates into excellent outcomes, too.

Lead with beauty and you win even if you lose. That's how I see it in those moments.

Unfortunately, it's not easy for me to hang onto that intention for more than a shot or point or two. Beauty is the sort of pleasure we partake of when we're not caught up in a struggle for survival. It's for our downtime, for our wine-and-sunset time. Importing it onto the field of battle is an interesting exercise, but it only works sometimes, and briefly.

Who or what inspires you to be your best on the tennis court?

#16: TO WHAT EXTENT DO THE FOLLOWING GET ACTIVATED WHEN YOU PLAY:
Beginner's Mind, Childish-Mind, Worried Mind?

The world we see is shaped by the lens we see it through. Beginner's Mind, Childish-Mind, and Worried Mind are lenses, filters that shape how we interpret the world.

You may be familiar with Beginner's Mind. The term, which comes out of the Zen tradition, refers to the innocence with which a person undertakes an activity for the first time, or as if it were the first time, because they aren't overlaying any narratives or expectations on the task. Because the activity isn't mediated, it's experienced more purely.

The best players in the world bring Beginner's Mind to their game. They are so steeped in technique that they let it all go when match time comes and execute with little or no noise in their head..

Childish-Mind, by contrast, has *only* noise in its head. It isn't something to aspire to. Childish-Mind is what happens when we get stuck inside the narratives that Beginner's Mind has no place for.*

I'll never beat him.

I can't hit my backhand down the line.

I always double-fault under pressure.

You want your Childish-Mind genie to stay locked in the

---

* Childish-Mind should not be confused with one's Inner Child, a New Age locution that evokes the innocent delight that many people believe are a hallmark of childhood.

bottle. It prejudices outcomes by emphasizing certainty over stroke-by-stroke, point-by-point performance. While it often manifests as the voice of failure and self-loathing, it can also err in the opposite direction and show up as hubris.

You'll never get up off the mat after you see me hit this shot!

You have to be really impressed by my service motion.

Whether it feeds your arrogance or insecurity, Childish-Mind bends your performance away from Beginner's Mind and toward failure.

On to the third character in our little triumvirate: Worried-Mind is the subpersonality that's so steeped in anxiety that it keeps us from having fun and performing with elan and delight. Like Childish-Mind, it shrouds us, but it's a shroud without a story — it's entirely biochemical. It's not the mindset we play our best from — it makes us hold our breath and execute tensely.

How often do you get to Beginner's Mind when you play? To what extent do you notice Child's Mind when it arises? What do you do about it when it does? Does Worried Mind ever drag you down, and if so, what do — and what can — you do about it?

#17. HOW LOUD IS YOUR MONKEY-MIND?

'Monkey mind' is a Buddhist concept. According to Google, it "refers to being unsettled, restless, or confused. ... It is also the part of your brain that becomes easily distracted."

Monkey Mind is how the vast majority of us operate virtually all the time. Our minds stay busy, and busy-ness means a lack of focus. I recall the late Larry King interviewing an allegedly enlightened guru on his television show. He fell silent for a moment, made a vague gesture in the general direction of the bearded sage, and then said in a tone that had both plaintiveness and wonder in it: "It's so still in there!"

Whereupon the guru answered, "It's that still in all of us. We just have to find it."

Meanwhile, back at the Monkey-Mind Ranch …

I haven't missed a return of serve all set. Or have I?

I shouldn't have missed that topspin lob.

Damn, that's a good-looking woman!

Monkey Mind's job isn't to be right. Monkey Mind's job is to be busy.

Monkey Mind can be useful when you practice, but only if it operates within the guard rails of the intention to get better at tennis. In that capacity, its busy-ness can be useful, especially if it's lateral. Competition is different. There, where the challenge is to clear the mind of extraneous thoughts and focus completely on the task at hand, Monkey Mind not only doesn't help — it defines the problem.

I cannot begin to count the number of times I've thought I was focusing well only to catch myself out musing about something irrelevant. *Should I change my shirt after this game or should I wait until the set is over? Where will I charge my car when the match is over and I head home?* Monkey Mind is one stubborn sumbitch. The most a person can reasonably hope to do is tamp down its volume and silence it for brief moments. It's not the sort of thing we completely outgrow.

How satisfied are you with the quality of attention you bring to your time on court?

#18: HOW GOOD ARE YOU AT PRACTICING SELF-FORGIVENESS ON THE TENNIS COURT?

Tennis can be a brutal game if you're not kind to yourself or — the next best thing — quickly forgetful. Over the course of a match, you'll have dozens if not hundreds of opportunities to get angry or frustrated with yourself. The shots you missed, the shots you could have played better, the extra effort you didn't make. The less you let these 'failures' get you down, the better off you'll be. You'll play better and you'll have more fun while you're doing it.

(Unless, of course, you're the sort of person who uses anger for fuel, in which case hating on yourself may not be a bad strategy.)

How deft are you at forgiving your trespasses?

#19: HOW IMPORTANT TO YOU IS THE PURSUIT OF EXCELLENCE RELATIVE TO THE STATUS QUO?

Cue the old joke: There are two types of people in the

world, those who divide the world into two types of people, and those who don't.

Which 'two types of people' is it this time? Those who live for the living, and those who live for the learning. Those who comfortably inhabit the status quo, and those who are always looking to push the envelope, always looking to get better. For some people, lifelong learning is a way of life. Others are mostly indifferent.

Most of us are a mix of the two. I am a mediocre cook at best, and the odds that I'll make a deep commitment to improving my stove game are close to zero despite the obvious rewards. When it comes to tennis, though, I'm a learn-aholic. I've authorized my obsessiveness to take over, so much so that here I am with a book about it!

We choose our battles, it's been said.

And, it seems, our pursuits of excellence, too.

Which camp does tennis fall into for you, 'fun status quo' or 'pursuit-of-mastery opportunity?' If it's a bit of both, how does that sort out percentage-wise? Are you happy with that ratio?

#20: ARE YOU DRAWN TO TENNIS AS A WISDOM PRACTICE?

Tennis is only one of a virtual infinity of potential wisdom practices. Here's a short, top-of-mind list of activities that open up the same learning opportunities.

Sex. Gardening. Hospice work. Marriage.

The world is your learning-opportunity oyster. How much, and in what ways, do you choose to dig in?

How do you feel about embracing tennis as a wisdom practice? Are you more drawn to other possible wisdom practices, and if so, what are they?

Fall Into Winter

I returned home from Philadelphia assuming my season was done. I'd achieved my goal of making it into the top ten, my hip was squawking, and no exciting opportunities were looming, with the possible exception of a major Category 2 event in Florida well down the road in late November.

More fundamentally, my attention was elsewhere. My wife Sheri Winston has been afflicted for decades with what has variously been called fibromyalgia and chronic fatigue syndrome. Her energy had been in decline for years, so much so that she'd stopped working a few years earlier. Now it had gotten so low that she literally couldn't sit up for more than an hour a day. Her energy battery was at about five on a scale of zero to 100.

Then a small miracle happened. Sheri is a well-known adult sex educator. A follower contacted her for a consultation, and when I advised her that my wife didn't have the energy for it, she recommended that we look into something called Proprioceptive Dysfunction Syndrome, also known as PDS. Apparently a Portuguese ophthalmologist named Orlando Alves da Silva had identified a systemic set of problems that arises when the eye muscles send wrong messages to the brain about how to navigate physical space. The brain learns to compensate, but at the cost of healthy neurological functioning. The result: A host of symptoms, many of which my wife checked off, including sleep issues, muscle spasms, fatigue, and double vision. The only reason Sheri's fan knew about this malady was because she was pursuing a master's in neuro-ophthalmology.

We were intrigued. My wife's double vision had come on recently — we thought it might be suggestive. We did more digging. Da Silva's pedigree was impressive. Eminent career, visiting professorships. He wasn't a quack — he was someone to take seriously. Although PDS was unknown in North America, he claimed to have treated 40,000 people over the last four decades in Europe with a 97% cure rate. Talk about a continental divide! We reached out to him, and he proved to be receptive, accommodating and, unlike many physicians, a real *mensch*.

We left for Lisbon in early September, about ten days after my return from Philadelphia. Our Portuguese adventure was an unqualified success. The good doctor confirmed my wife's diagnosis and equipped her with what she promptly dubbed "magic glasses" that corrected her neuro-ophthalmological misfiring and *immediately* boosted her energy level from five to about twenty. She wasn't cured, not by a long shot, but it would take months if not years to rewire her brain after all those decades carving out misbegotten pathways. Thanks to Orlando da Silva, she was on her way.

We got to enjoy Lisbon within the limits of her modest energy. The weather, the water, the hills, the mix of old and new, the views — we fell in love immediately. It was like San Francisco with a whole lot of Europe thrown in. Since Orlando da Silva is basically the only doctor in the world who knows about PDS, we will be going there again. Talk about a happy obligation!

LONGMEADOW, MA

Once we were home, my thoughts turned to tennis again. My hip was feeling better and I was now ranked sixth in the country — it might be fun to try to boost that ranking. There was a tournament coming up in early October, the Clem Easton Memorial in Longmeadow MA. As a Category Four event, it might attract tough competition, which is to say *fun* competition – and if I did well, I would accumulate enough points to boost my ranking.

I registered for the tournament — my wife felt well enough to travel with me. It was a small draw and I was the top seed. Assuming I won, there'd be two matches before the finals.

Longmeadow is directly north of Hartford just across the Connecticut border. The venue for the tournament, the Field Club of Longmeadow, is a sprawling setup with a long drive-way and twelve green Har-Tru courts arranged in three sets of four, on either side of a long walkway.

Supersenior tennis attracts all sorts. My first Clem Easton opponent seemed physically unable to have two balls on his person at any time. When he served, he'd hold one ball, hit his serve, and then, if he missed it, go fetch a second ball and serve that one. He expressed real concern when I ignored a ball sitting on my side of the court — I assumed it offended his sense of order. He grunted and howled randomly when chasing a shot — I couldn't detect any relationship whatsoever between his vocalizations and his physical effort. I beat him 6-0, 6-0 and it wasn't that close.

Next up, a more middle-of-the-bell-curve guy named Jay Lubker who ran a commercial glass business when he wasn't playing tennis. He was ranked twenty-eighth in the country, which might or might not mean something given the unreliability of USTA rankings. Jay had beaten Ed Paige in three sets in the first round. This was the same Ed Paige I'd barely beaten in the Newburgh semis, so I figured I'd be in for a struggle.

Jay proved to be one of those guys who gets the most out of a somewhat unorthodox game. He played right-handed but appeared to be ambidextrous. He warmed up hitting a two-handed forehand only to abandon that technique when the match started. There was also that time when I threw up a lob to his backhand and he put it away with a left-handed overhead. The first set was a tussle — I scraped by 6-4. His play slacked off in the second and I played better as I grew more confident. The final score was 6-4, 6-1.

At this point, I made what would prove to be a tactical mistake. I'd played Jay on a Saturday — the finals were scheduled for Sunday. I had a hankering to get home and not spend another night in a motel, so I proposed to Jon Wilson, my finals opponent, that we double-dip and play the final the same day. I wasn't being serious, but he liked the idea and was game to proceed if the tournament officials were willing.

They were. I decided to proceed. I was probably in as good shape as Jon, if not better, and why not get it over with?

I'd seen Wilson play at the Category 3 tournament in Guilford, where he'd been bounced in the semi-finals by Lloyd Clareman. He had lovely strokes, but he hadn't been moving well that day. I hoped to run him around and beat him that way.

Jon was ranked #16 nationally, but what did that mean? A lot, as things turned out. I played pretty well, but lost anyway. The scores were 5-7, 6-1, 6-2. At 4-2, 30-0 in the final set, I pulled up with a yelp. My body had run out of glycogen and my left hamstring was letting me know. I played out the match knowing I couldn't win because he deserved to win with a full line score, not by retirement.

Full credit to Wilson: He made very few errors and wore me down with a combination of drives deep to the backhand and drop shots to my forehand. When I asked the Longmeadow pro in attendance for a critique, he said, "He controlled the court better than you." That was the explanation in a nutshell. Jon had me on a string for the last two sets.

I came away from the match with some clear lessons.

Get my return of serve deeper so my opponent wouldn't start his service points in an offensive posture.

Disguise my intentions better.

Play from on, not behind, the baseline.

Make sensible decisions about how much to tax your body.

Although I didn't win the tournament, I did accomplish

my other mission. When the new rankings came out a few days later, I had climbed to #3.

TORRINGTON, CT

Once I got home, a new notion took root in me. I didn't have to stop now. I was only a few points behind the second-ranked player. If I did well in a local tournament, even a low-level one, and he remained idle, I could leapfrog him to number two. Not only that, but Gary Jenkins, who had a pretty massive lead at #1, hadn't signed up for the big Longboat Key tournament, which I'd been tracking. If he'd actually hung up his sneakers for the year, and if I won a couple of easy local tournaments and also reached the semis at Longboat Key, I could end up at number one!

It was very tempting. I'd set out to make it into the top ten, and now I was looking at a clear if by no means certain path to number one. But I was also disinclined. It felt a bit unseemly, for one thing. By now, I knew all too well how misleading the national rankings could be. There were guys ranked in the top 30 who wouldn't be able to beat me on their best day and my worst one. I'd be exploiting the 'points for playing' loophole — in short, I'd be juking the stats.

I wouldn't be breaking any rules, though, so why not go for it? This is what my friends and family, who seemed prouder of my lofty ranking than I was, kept telling me. I didn't require much persuading and decided to go with the flow.

A few days before registration closed, I signed up for a

Level 5 tournament in Torrington, CT, a ninety-minute drive away. It looked like easy pickings. Only two people other than myself had registered, my OCD opponent from Longmeadow and a fellow named Peter Longsho, who was revealed after a bit of research to be over 75 with a track record that appeared to pose no threat. But then, literally minutes before registrations closed, Jay Lubker signed up, too. He'd beaten Jon Wilson recently, and although I'd beaten Jay in straight sets at the Clem Easton Memorial, that meant he could beat me, too.

Meanwhile Gary Jenkins had signed up for Longboat Key, ending my fantasy about ending the year at number one. No matter: I'd keep my commitment to play the Torrington tournament — and probably head down to Florida, too. The Torrington draw was tiny — I'd have two matches at most. If I got through my first round, my ranking would climb to #2.

The tournament director scheduled both matches for the same day. As a rule, this is problematic for supersenior players, one match typically being more than enough. I was okay with his decision though. The first match would be easy; I'd basically be playing one match, plus.

It ended up being one match, period. Peter Longsho didn't show and never bothered to call in about it, leaving me to hang out in a dingy lobby for a couple of hours while Jay Lubker disposed of his opponent.

The facility where we played was tired. The courts played too fast to be much fun, and on half a dozen occasions we had to take a towel and clean up spots on the court where moisture had leached through the roof. I won a straightforward victory, with Jay winning one more game than he had the previous time we played.

And there I was when the new ratings came out, up to number two, eliciting impressed noises from friends and family while I walked around as conscious of my juking as I was of my ranking.

LONGBOAT KEY, FL

After a quiet Thanksgiving, my wife and I headed south to Longboat Key, FL on the Gulf Coast where I'd be playing in the season finale, a big Category 2 tournament — a virtual national tournament, really — that in 2021 drew over 400 participants from around the country in divisions ranging from 55 to 85, with a full draw of 64 in the 70's.

Ah, Florida. The Longboat Key area, like so much of the state, is at the intersection of Jimmy Buffetville and God's waiting room. Lots of wrinkles, lots of booze, set in a landscape of sea, sand, condos, tiki bars, golf courses — and, of course, tennis courts, which you can scarcely turn a corner without seeing.

It was clear when I arrived why folks take planes to play here. The weather was perfect, cool at night and climbing to around 70 during the day. The green Har-Tru courts were impeccable. There are so many competitors that the tournament is played at multiple venues in addition to the main one, a ten-court complex with a two-story viewing area.

This was my fourth trip to a Level 3 or higher event. I was getting to know this interesting community. More than a few of the better players had been number one on their college teams. Others had had full tennis-industry careers. One fellow I chatted with at Longboat Key runs a tennis training center in California. Jim Nelson, whom I'd beaten in the finals at Newburgh earlier this year, was a teaching pro in Ohio as well as the traveling companion on the world tour of his sister Vicki Nelson, who was a top 100 player — and whose lingering renown is for having played the longest point in the history of recorded competitive tennis, a whopping 643 shots. (No typo.) Vishnu Maharaj, about whom more below, ran tennis operations at a big resort in Georgia and had also been the facilities manager at Crandon Park in Miami, where a big ATP 1000 event is held.

So: Studs, careerists, anomalies like myself — the once and future tennis player — and, of course, the usual assortment of guys who play out of love of the game and for the camaraderie. The great equalizer, of course, is time. Not only do you have to know how to play to do well at the supersenior level, you also need the body to do it with. And aging is kind to us differently.

I came into the tournament ranked second in the country and hoping not to be seeded at that lofty level. I don't particularly enjoy being the center of attention — I'd rather surprise people than have a target on my back. Integrity was a consideration for me, too. I didn't merit that seeding, despite my ranking. An 'all-factors' approach was used for seeding at the Longboat Key tournament — ranking, historical performance, opponent caliber, and more. I was seeded ninth, with a bunch of other guys. (Individuals were assigned the first four seeds, four guys were lumped at five, and seven of us at nine.) This suited me fine. It felt like that was where I belonged, and it also probably meant a kinder draw than if I weren't seeded.

My first-round opponent was a guy named Sonny Perkins. The draw listed him as coming from Alabama, but he also had a residence in the Sarasota area, so this was a home game for him. He didn't have the game to compete with me, as he himself acknowledged when we were done. I won 6-1, 6-2 without playing particularly well. It was only in the early part of the second set that I felt able to execute at the level I expect of myself, fluidly and competently.

Next up: Mark Morales from Kentucky. Short, athletic-looking, packing a few extra pounds but maybe not enough to slow him down. He'd won his first match love and love, which spelled possible danger. I expected him to pose a real challenge, all the more so when we started to warm up. He had a solid forehand and reminded me briefly of Jon Wilson, who'd defeated me in the Longmeadow final in October. But then I noticed that he had trouble handling balls deep to his backhand, and when he came to the net, I sensed real uncertainty there. The match was over quickly, a good thing because if it had gone on for much over an hour, we'd have bumped up against twilight and had to continue the next day. The final score was six-love, six-one. I was very happy with how I'd played. When it was over, Mark asked me, "Do you ever miss?"

Our contest was a great example of how a matchup can make you look very good or very bad. Morales's strengths and weaknesses were tailor-made for my game. He was a step slow, which made the court look very big (and made me more confident), and his ground strokes set up perfectly for me.

I had the next day off, and welcomed it. I wanted to find a practice court and work on my serve, which was acting unreliable. Perhaps the only downside of this tournament is the virtual absence of practice courts. The vast majority of all those courts one sees are owned by private condo complexes, which are disinclined to let a gaggle of geezers descend like locusts onto their Har-Tru. I did some googling and found three public courts ten minutes north of Bradenton Beach, where my wife and I were staying.

I set up on an end court and started practicing. A few minutes later, two long and lean young women took the other end court. At first, I thought they were in high school, but that is only because I'm older than Methuselah. They started off playing short-court and I noted with interest that they seemed to have a clue. They moved to the backcourt and it was clear they had more than a clue. They had gorgeous strokes — in addition to being gorgeous — and they hit the ball hard. For all I knew, they were products of the world-famous IMG tennis factory, which was just across the bridge and down the road.

I strolled over and introduced myself. One of the benefits of being ranked second in the country, merited or not, is that it makes this sort of "Hello, I'm here" approach easier to pull off. It also helped that I could have been their granddad. They probably wouldn't think I was hitting on them.

It turned out that they were college-age. One of them played varsity at the University of Hawaii, and the other would have been playing Division One tennis but for shoulder surgery. They graciously invited me to hit with them and I did just that, holding my own for a fun ten minutes before heading back to my court to work on my serve again.

I did so feeling blessed. How often does one happen onto a public court only to find reasonable facsimiles of the young Anna Kournikova and Ana Ivanova banging the ball two courts down? Maybe my luck would carry over to the next day and my round of sixteen match. There'd be a real charge to the match — that much I already knew. My opponent was a guy named Joe Bouquin. It was a name I remembered from back in the day when he'd been a feared player, a real force in the East. This match would bring up all my old insecurities: Noone against Someone, Imposter against Actual Player, Nerd-in-the-Corner against Big-Kid-on-Campus.

I'd done some preliminary research on Joe, knowing I might meet him down the road. The report: He had super-solid ground strokes, but time was having its way with him. He had vision issues — glaucoma in one eye, he told me later — and he was slowing down a bit. I watched him play for a few minutes and noted an odd habit when he played. He'd often grunt, howl or even yowl when pursuing a ball. Concerned about getting distracted, I spoke with a USTA official who told me that there was nothing in the rules prohibiting his vocalizations unless they impinged on his opponent's ability to concentrate when it came time to hit the ball. That didn't appear to be an issue. I resolved to disregard his hollering.

My match with him was the weirdest one I've ever played. I started slowly — I could feel my neuroses casting a small shadow. I got over that after three or four games, but my play remained erratic. I kept missing, often by a tiny margin. A wind was blowing just hard enough to make a difference, and maybe it was one of those days. My second serve abandoned me completely. It's very unsettling to launch into your motion without a clue as to where the ball will land.

Still, it was a match. Joe, who as advertised had impeccable groundstrokes, went up 4-1 and ended up winning the first set 6-3 "fairly easily," as per his own characterization postmatch to someone on the far end of his cellphone.

It soon became evident that Joe was immensely uncomfortable at the net. It wasn't his technique, which was spot-on stem to stern — it was his vision. I didn't need to figure this out on my own. Early on, I hit a short lob, he dinked it back, I won the point, and he cried out, "I can't see it!"

If he was going to beat me, it would have to be from the backcourt. He wouldn't be able to sneak up to net on me.

Along about the end of the first set, Bouquin yowled in pain and collapsed onto the court. He'd strained his upper left quad. Compassionate soul that I am, I immediately started running him as much as I could. I must have done a good job because half a dozen or more times over the course of the next set, he yelped after a point and collapsed onto the court, sometimes spread-eagled completely. One time, he hollered from his place on the Har-Tru, "Will you stop running me so much?"

Every time this happened, he got up and played the next point like he was just fine. If you were to see a video of just the points we played, you'd never know he was injured or exhausted.

I wasn't annoyed, I was entertained. On one occasion with him down for a nine-count, I turned to the gaggle of people watching and said, "Is this a tennis match or a melodrama?" Whereupon the USTA official on duty chimed in, "Next show: Three o'clock."

Bouquin went up 5-3 in the second set. It felt like the beginning of the end. Illicit thoughts like "Well, it's not a totally unrespectable score" were running through my head. Then I held serve: 5-4. I was still in it!

At the changeover, the chatty USTA official said, "You guys are killing it!"

I looked at him in disbelief. My second serve had gotten so unreliable that I was serving underhanded, which Bouquin couldn't take advantage of because of his vision (and volleying) issues. He'd chip and charge, I'd lob deep, he'd play it back as a ground stroke, and only then would the point begin in earnest.

"In effort," the USTA official elaborated. "These points are crazy. You've been out here for over two hours."

I hadn't realized. A few of our points had left me heaving for breath, but two hours-plus of tennis for eighteen games without any meaningful delays — his court collapses were frequent but brief — meant we'd been playing really long points.

Joe had been a gentleman throughout. I said to the USTA official (but really to Joe, who was sitting down the bench from me), "The normal guy who strained his thigh would have defaulted by now."

Bouquin answered: "Never."

Back onto the court. He goes up 30-0. *Uh-oh.* My turn to step up: I hit three perfect shots on the next point concluding with a backhand volley down the line to get to 30-15, then scrape my way back to 30-all. He wins the next point: 40-30. Match point! He misses his first serve. What to do? I decide to go for it. I'm pissed off at how I've played (that horrific serve!) and figure I might as well go out in style.

His second serve comes to my forehand. I hit my return close to perfectly, a big inside-out forehand that takes him wide, and follow it to net. *Make him win it!!* He goes down the line with his backhand and it lands a few inches wide. It's way too early to exult. But then I win the next two points and it's 5-5.

The match is now a virtual toss-up or even slightly in my favor. If I can somehow pull out the set, which is no sure thing, I'll probably be able to outlast him in the finale. He's the one who's been moaning and collapsing, after all. I'm at the net picking up a ball when he comes up to the net and sticks out his hand.

I look at him in disbelief. This was the guy who only minutes before had said, "Default? Never!"

"I'm done," he says now. "The muscle strain isn't the problem. It's mild. But I've got nothing left in my quads. They're gone."

3-6, 5-5, retire. I was into the quarter-finals!

It was hours before my victory fully registered. I'd been looking uphill virtually from the first point. Even after getting level in the second set, it had been far from clear that I'd win the match. It was a legitimate win, though, as my tennis friend Doug Grunther, who'd played Bouquin back in the day, reminded me. A victory by TKO.

My quarter-final opponent was Vishnu Maharaj, a lifelong tennis guy with an estimable reputation on the senior circuit. He was, I was told, a deft touch player in the Indian tradition, all feel, angles and disguise. It sounded like a fun challenge.

I'd spoken with Vishnu briefly on the first day of the tournament. He was congenial, soft-spoken, gracious. On court, though, he was all business, inturned and 100% focused on the business of winning. There'd be no chatty repartee with him today. "It's the Maharaj way," someone told me later. "His brother" — also a high-level supersenior player — "does the same."

According to one source, Vishnu had been playing tournaments virtually every weekend for his entire life. His experience showed — he gave me a crash course in senior tennis. Virtually every ground stroke he hit was a slice. Not the sort of floating slice that sits up and lets the opponent take a good whack at it, but a crisp slice that bit and scooted upon impact. Because his ball stayed low, he neutralized my topspin forehand, which is my best weapon. His disguise was impeccable. Because he always set up with the racket high, it was impossible to read when he'd drop and when he'd drive. Brent Abel had told me a few weeks earlier that disguise is the name of the game in senior tennis — Vishnu proved him right. Early in the second set, I mildly strained my hamstring when I read drop shot, got my weight going forward, and then had to pivot hard to the left to chase down a slice deep to my backhand. It was a repetitive motion injury — the sequence had already befallen me multiple times.

Vishnu was impressively precise. When I play, I go for the territory. He went for the spot, or seemed to. His movement showed his age, but he compensated for this with good hip flexibility that allowed him to return balls that were mostly behind him. I probably got passed half a dozen times on points that I was already putting in my column. He also read me like the proverbial book — the result, I think, of a life spent on the tennis court (him) and an unfortunate tendency to skywrite intentions (me). Bottom line, the dude could play.

It wasn't a rout. I lost 6-2, 6-4, and I was up 4-3, 40-15 in the second set. If I'd won one of the next two points, who knows what might have happened? But that's when my serve, which had behaved itself in the first set, got up on its hind legs and bitch-slapped me. The next thing I knew, I was down 5-4, 40-0. I sliced a down-the-line backhand wide and the match was over.

His off-court congeniality returned when the match was over. "You'd be a hellacious practice partner," he said. "You chase lots of balls down."

I gratefully accepted the compliment. Desperate egos grasp for small straws, right? I left the court frustrated at my performance — again, I wasn't happy with my play — but Vishnu had made me play badly.

A few days later, I spoke with a friend who knows Vishnu's game and he said, "I think you could beat him." That was bracing — and also, I believe, true. I'd need to bring my A game, though. I'd also need to disguise my shots better, which could come with focused practice. But he was the better player on this day.

Maharaj ended up winning the tournament. His semi-final victory was a straightforward four and three victory. In the finals, he played a guy named Tom Jaklitsch with whom I'd gotten friendly over the course of the tournament. The owner of multiple tennis clubs on Long Island, Tom had played number three at Cornell — his game reminded me stylistically and strategically of my own. He'd played a three and a half hour match the day before against Gary Jenkins, the number one seed, which he'd won when Gary's calf crapped out on him early in the final set. Tom had strained a hamstring during the same match and came out taped up and exhausted for the match against Vishnu. The final score was 6-4, 6-5, retire. Tom had set points in the second set, failed to close the set out, and quit because, like Joe Bouquin against me a few days earlier, he was burned out. Done.

I flew home feeling good overall about how I'd done at the tournament. Without playing my best, I'd justified my seeding (and then some) by advancing to the final eight of a major quasi-national tournament. I'd had two straightforward wins and one wacky win that could be attributed, at least in part, to my pluck and persistence. I'd also been shown a template (thanks, Vishnu!) for how to be more fearsome against my geriatric peers. I'd traveled to Longboat Key to find out if I genuinely belonged in the upper tier of the supersenior 70s division. I returned home more convinced than ever that I did.

Supersenior tennis is a game of conditioning, of strategy, and of attrition. In tournaments with big draws, withdrawals become likelier, if not plain likely, as the damage accumulates. At the Philadelphia grass nationals, David Sivertson won the semi-finals when Bob Litwin retired after one set. At Longboat Key, Vishnu Maharaj won a close final via mid-match retirement.

At the end of the day, and toward the back end of a life, playing supersenior tennis inevitably becomes a meditation on mortality. Every competitor is, in their own way, raging against the dying of the light. I headed home from Longboat Key in a slightly melancholy mood. Two cornerstones of the supersenior circuit, Mas Kimball and Larry Turville, had died in recent months — a photo of Turville, whom I'd never met, had graced the registration area. I hadn't played my best and I was feeling physically dinged. I was feeling afflicted by the sense that my peers and I weren't playing tennis matches, we were engaging in wars of attrition — and every one of us would lose in the end. Were we all wasting our time?

My wife and I got to Newark Airport, recharged our car, and headed back to Kingston. My spirits perked up as I got the scent of the stable. If tennis is a wisdom practice, I asked myself, what can it teach us about death? I was on a quest of sorts, and quests always start with a question. This must have been a good one, because my mind promptly came up with an answer. The notion that we're in competition with death was one possible narrative among many — it was, in this sense, optional. Why not come up with an equally true and more congenial story? What if death wasn't an enemy? What if we positioned death not as a problem, but as a partner and a friend?

Logically, this view made at least as much sense as the death-as-enemy narrative. Life is literally inconceivable without the concept of death. You can have love without marriage, despite what the song says, but you can't have life without death — it's the shadow side of the coin.

There now popped into my head a new image.

A new movie.

I'm on the court playing a supersenior tennis match against a faceless guy in his 70s, a sort of twin of myself.

Death is watching, a gentle approving spirit, not at all hostile or menacing. He's in the shadows and seated quietly. He's there to celebrate and why wouldn't he? He's Life's life partner; he adores Her. He's rooting equally for the two contestants. He delights in the dance — he admires our commitment and persistence. Death appreciates all things beautiful.

On the court, we're aching, we're wincing, we're moving much slower than we used to. Yet we manage, on occasion, to impress.

I chase down a drop shot and flick it away.

The guy across the net gives me a big thumb's up.

From the shadows, Death applauds.

I pick up a ball and head back to the baseline. It's time for the next point.

Focus. Breathe. Play it like it's your last point ever.

And then I keep plugging away.

Epilogue

As I write these words, it is the dead of winter. An ice storm has shut down Kingston. My return to the supersenior circuit, if it happens, is a few months away.

Will I do it? Probably — but not certainly. Over the last months, I've found myself wondering if this book was the real reason I started playing supersenior tennis. As I noted in the Introduction, that's been a pattern in my life — I decide to do something and end up writing about it.

Life is full of things to do and write about. I recently entered local politics — maybe my next book will be about that. I'm also considering a deeper dive into aging and elderhood. Or maybe the book that the world badly needs about Proprioceptive Dysfunction Syndrome?

A sequel is appealing, though. If I could get all the way up to number two this year, might number one await me in 2022, or maybe even a national title?

It's a tempting aspiration.

What would it take to get the 10-20% better that would give me a real shot at a national title? It's an interesting question, one that's already producing answers that have to do with off-court conditioning and adding more muscularity to my game.

Tennis as a Wisdom Practice, Part Deux: A Story About a

Quest for a National Title.

I like the idea. I like it a lot. But maybe not so much as to actually do it.

Time will tell, time which rules until it doesn't.

Tomorrow is another day — until tomorrow isn't.

If you liked this book,
please consider posting a
review on Amazon

TinyUrl.com/carltennis

Thank you!

Made in the USA
Middletown, DE
17 May 2022

65882078R00099